BEARING FRUIT
—— OR ——
LIVING BARREN

The Essentials of Christian Spirituality

Preston Condra

Kelly Condra

Bearing Fruit or Living Barren
The Essentials of Christian Spirituality
Preston Condra and Kelly Condra
Sufficient Word Publishing

Published by Sufficient Word Publishing, Springdale, AR
Copyright ©2018 Preston Condra and Kelly Condra

Back cover photography: Linda Richards, lindarichardsphotography.com

Cover and Interior design: Davis Creative, DavisCreative.com

Library of Congress Cataloging-in-Publication Data
Library of Congress Control Number: 2018905468
Preston Condra and Kelly Condra

Bearing Fruit or Living Barren: The Essentials of Christian Spirituality
ISBN: 978-1-946245-06-9
Library of Congress subject headings:
1. REL012120 RELIGION / Christian Life / Spiritual Growth
2. REL006220 RELIGION / Biblical Studies / New Testament
3. REL006700 RELIGION / Biblical Studies / Bible Study Guides

2018

For if these things be in you, and abound,

they make you that ye shall *neither* be

barren nor unfruitful in the knowledge

of our Lord Jesus Christ.

(2 Peter 1:8)

Table of Contents

Introduction   Thinking Differently About the Christian Life...... 1

Chapter 1   The Natural Man 7

Chapter 2   The Spiritual Man............................ 17

Chapter 3   The Carnal Man 29

Chapter 4   Living Barren by Quenching the Spirit........... 43

Chapter 5   Living Barren by Grieving the Spirit............. 55

Chapter 6   The Filling of the Spirit 65

Chapter 7   The Character of Fruit......................... 71

Chapter 8   Who Can Be Known By Their Fruits?............ 87

Conclusion   Here, Enjoy Some Fruit........................ 93

THINKING DIFFERENTLY ABOUT THE CHRISTIAN LIFE

See that ye refuse not him that speaketh. (Hebrews 12:25a)

Many Christians greatly desire to obey God. They willingly share their faith, serve others, and study God's word. Some, however, feel disconnected from the descriptions of joy, peace and contentment which should accompany their dutiful service. They might wonder, "How could Peter be serving happily when that service included suffering? How could Paul sing hymns in prison? How could Christians walk bravely and gladly to martyrdom when I can't even smile my way through a workday?"

As do many saints today, the brave martyrs of history gave thanks during trials and did things they never thought they could because they learned to be spiritual, meaning to emanate the things of the Spirit. The joy they displayed in adversity was the character of God shining through them. The Christian who believes God and yields to His purpose allows God's grace to produce godliness, strength and service, all to God's glory. Such a Christian is cooperating with God's spiritual program and is therefore Spirit-filled. He is literally filled up with the power and goodness of God, and the result is spiritual fruit.

Many who read this book are already doing the things described herein; they read God's word, exercise faith, and rely on God for many things. Not all, however, will have combined these aspects of Christian living for the purpose of being Spirit-filled. Church attendance and Christian service are also well-practiced among God's people, but not every Christian knows that he is to discern his spiritual condition as a necessary part of bearing fruit. Worship and good works that are pleasing to God are a by-product of spirituality. Learning to be spiritual is not saying to oneself, "I need to work harder on that." It is saying, "I can do these things because He can. He does it all if I just say, 'Yes.'"

"Saying 'Yes' to God" is a simplified description of the "how-to" of spirituality. To paraphrase the writer of Hebrews, it is a mindset of "not refusing Him." Spirituality is not a to-do list. It is an attitude and a way of thinking. It says, "Yes, I want to know you; yes, I want to know your word. I want to do your will, and I am willing to be made willing. Yes, I will sacrifice things of this world in favor of things of eternal value. And, yes, I know you are not a big meanie and therefore I need not fear saying, 'Yes.'"

Spirituality is a mindset wholly informed by God's word. Spirit-filled living is possible when a Christian makes its teachings the primary focus of his mind. Doing so leads to changes in attitude, motive, choices and behaviors. If one is literally filled up with good and righteous and holy things, there is less likelihood of ungodliness, and more potential for fruitfulness.

God desires that his children bear much fruit. To bear fruit means to be productive in one's Christian life, but productivity is not simply being busy; the fruit of righteousness is of a particular quality which can only come from God Himself. Fruitfulness is allowing the Holy Spirit to produce His spiritual fruit within, so that all things are done with a godly motive and with God's character displayed in the process.

Unbelievers can do good deeds, but only one who is born again can produce genuine godly character and the virtues of Jesus Christ.

From godly character comes the fruit of righteousness: godly choices and Christian service. Although this book focuses on the spiritual prerequisite to good works, we do not minimize the importance of sharing the Gospel with the unsaved, and serving, helping, comforting, teaching and giving to the needs of the body of Christ. We simply want to make it abundantly clear that a Christian's works are a sweet-smelling sacrifice only when they are a product of spirituality.

Whether or not a Christian bears fruit that pleases God depends wholly upon his spiritual condition. If he cannot recognize his condition and make the necessary adjustments, he will not be consistently spiritual nor bear much fruit. He might be busy with religious activity, but he will be doing so by his own power. Therefore, it is worth noting that the various aspects of spirituality are not "steps" to spirit-filled living, but descriptive elements of things that are in practice when spirituality is maintained. Consider how fruit-bearing works on a fruit tree. The farmer does not "make" fruit; he provides the environment for a tree to be fruitful. With sun, water and good soil, fruit is the natural product of a tree. Similarly, as Christians we do not set out to make fruit; we operate in an environment of truth, faith and reliance upon God, and fruitfulness is the result.

The condition of being spiritual and its outworking, known as "walking in the Spirit," is an enablement given to the church; it allows the members of the body of Christ to know the deep things of God, to access the power of God's grace, and to use that power to properly apply the truths learned. It is not enough to be aware of spiritual truth; in order to maintain his spiritual walk, a Christian must understand it, believe it, and actively limit his thinking to exclude things which draw him away from the truth. Spirituality is an active and dynamic volitional element within our relationship to God: we decide day-by-day, sometimes moment-by-moment whether or not we will cooperate with God.

Spirituality is a large subject; it is, in general, the topic of all the epistles to the church. Spirituality is the way in which God expects us to deal with everything, no matter how important or how trivial it may be. It is the way that we access every blessing, defeat every foe, understand God's word and recognize how to apply His truths to our lives. Spirituality is vital to walking in freedom from the Christian's three spiritual enemies. Its elements include recognizing and refusing carnality, controlling one's thought life, and operating by faith rather than using external laws and rules to control behavior. When a Christian stumbles in his walk, spirituality is regained by a change of mind that confesses agreement with God.

Because the premise of this book is to encourage Christians to think a little differently about Christian living, we, the authors, chose to explain some things without using the most commonly known wording. Sometimes the most-often used phraseology is easy to rapidly brush over; an informed reader may feel he understands faith, for example, and will spend little time considering it further. Less commonly used explanations might shed new light or even explain some things better. For example, what is commonly known as the sin nature, we refer to as the sin principle, or law of sin, as Paul did. Doing so helps to explain sinfulness as a volitional way of operating. In order to distinguish faith from a nebulous mental exercise or wishful thinking, we describe it as directing one's faith. This reminds readers that faith is a choice and requires an object. We use the term "faith system" to distinguish Christian living from Israel's law system, and also to emphasize that **how** we do God's will is vital, arguably more so than what we do. We hope that our readers find the language adequately explanatory, helpful and thought-provoking.

Those who know us know that our greatest desire is that every Christian becomes well-versed in explaining the Gospel of Christ, 1 Corinthians 15:1-4, and that they do so regularly. Our second greatest passion is for each member of the body of Christ to be energized by the Spirit of God to meet his full potential to the glory of our Lord Jesus Christ, who so richly deserves the crowns we will lay at His feet.

And they departed from the presence of the council, rejoicing that they were counted worthy to suffer shame for his name. (Acts 5:41)

If we live in the Spirit, let us also walk in the Spirit. (Galatians 5:25)

See then that ye walk circumspectly, not as fools, but as wise, Redeeming the time, because the days are evil. Wherefore be ye not unwise, but understanding what the will of the Lord is. (Ephesians 5:15-17)

*Every branch in me that beareth not fruit he taketh away: and every branch that beareth **fruit**, he purgeth it, that it may bring forth **more fruit**. ... I am the vine, ye are the branches: He that abideth in me, and I in him, the same bringeth forth **much fruit**: for without me ye can do nothing.* (John 15:2, 5, emphasis added)

But I have all, and abound: I am full, having received of Epaphroditus the things which were sent from you, an odour of a sweet smell, a sacrifice acceptable, wellpleasing to God. (Philippians 4:18)

Moreover, brethren, I declare unto you **the gospel** *which I preached unto you, which also ye have received, and wherein ye stand;* **By which also ye are saved**, *if ye keep in memory what I preached unto you, unless ye have believed in vain. For I delivered unto you first of all that which I also received, how that Christ died for our sins according to the scriptures; And that he was buried, and that he rose again the third day according to the scriptures: And that he was seen of Cephas, then of the twelve: After that, he was seen of above five hundred brethren at once; of whom the greater part remain unto this present, but some are fallen asleep. After that, he was seen of James; then of all the apostles. And last of all he was seen of me also, as of one born out of due time.* (1 Corinthians 15:1-8, emphasis added)

Chapter 1

THE NATURAL MAN

The Bible teaches that there are three possibilities as to the spiritual condition of man. These conditions are described as three kinds of men: the natural man, the spiritual man and the carnal man. Two of these kinds of men are saved; they have believed the Gospel of Christ, 1 Corinthians 15:1-4, and have been spiritually born again. The two possible conditions of a saved man are that he is either spiritual or carnal. A spiritual man is living the way God intends: by the power of the Holy Spirit. A carnal man is one who is living by a different source of energizing power. He is operating by the principle of sin which dwells within his body, and he is therefore functioning as if he is unsaved. The natural man is the third kind of man described in the Bible. He is unsaved, and because of his spiritual condition, he is not able under any circumstances to produce spirituality. He is the topic of this chapter.

What is a Natural Man?

The natural man is Paul's descriptive title for those who are unsaved. This man is "natural" because he remains in the condition in which he was born; separated from God, dead in trespasses and sins, and destined for eternity in the lake of fire. His condition can only change if he comes to believe the Gospel of Christ for his eternal salvation, excluding all other means, methods or additions. The natural man cannot walk by faith and cannot please God. He is not "good" in

God's estimation, but is instead an enemy of God. He may not know it himself, but the natural man is totally under the power of the sin principle which operates within him. The sin principle, also called the "law of sin" in Romans, is commonly known as the sin nature. It is a way of operating and a source of inspiration and power, similar to the way that obeying the laws of this world is a way of operating in life. The natural man is not able to operate in any other way because he is "free from righteousness." Albeit unintentionally, the natural man is also working in cooperation with Satan and his world system. Everything that he does, although it may not be evil, immoral, or illegal, is of a quality that is equivalent to sin because it is not produced by the righteousness of God.

> *For when ye were the servants of sin, ye were free from righteousness.* (Romans 6:20)

The natural man is in the family of Adam and is not part of the family of God nor the body of Christ. He was **generated** by fallen parents who were generated by fallen parents all the way back to Adam and Eve. Whether the natural man attends church, reads the Bible or serves is of no consequence. Only the **regeneration** of a spiritual birth changes the condition, position, and destination of a natural man. The situation of the natural man may seem bleak because God is righteous and He justly punishes sin. God, however, is also love. Because of that great love, God the Son took upon Himself humanity and offered Himself to God the Father as the recipient of the penalty for the sins of the world. Christ's death as a payment for sin was as a substitute for all mankind. God provides every opportunity for man to know Him and to be saved by Christ's sacrifice. The natural man is rightly separated from a holy God and will remain so if he does not accept the gracious payment which was made on his behalf. Eventually he will face the wrath of God against sin. This is God's estimation of the natural man:

> *As it is written, There is none righteous, no, not one: There is none*
> *that understandeth, there is none that seeketh after God. They*
> *are all gone out of the way, they are together become unprofitable;*
> *there is none that doeth good, no, not one.* (Romans 3:10-12)

The Destiny of the Natural Man

The Bible is clear about the destiny of the natural man. If he does not accept the payment for sin made by Jesus Christ, he himself will pay God's penalty for his sins:

> *Let no man deceive you with vain words: for because of these*
> *things cometh the wrath of God upon the children of disobedience.*
> (Ephesians 5:6)

> *And I saw the dead, small and great, stand before God; and the*
> *books were opened: and another book was opened, which is the*
> *book of life: and the dead were judged out of those things which*
> *were written in the books, according to their works. And the sea*
> *gave up the dead which were in it; and death and hell delivered*
> *up the dead which were in them: and they were judged every*
> *man according to their works. And death and hell were cast into*
> *the lake of fire. This is the second death. And whosoever was not*
> *found written in the book of life was cast into the lake of fire.*
> (Revelation 20:12-15)

The Destiny of God's Children

The children of God are those who have accepted Christ's sacrificial death on the cross for their sins by believing the Gospel of Christ. They are children because they have been spiritually born into God's family. The physical death and spiritual punishment of Christ was a satisfying sacrifice to God for the sins of the world. It was sufficient for any and all sins, and therefore, in contrast to the destiny of the natural man, God's children are saved from the penalty of sin. They have no appointment with the wrath of God:

> *Much more then, being now justified by his blood, we shall be saved from wrath through him.* (Romans 5:9)

> *And to wait for his Son from heaven, whom he raised from the dead, even Jesus, which delivered us from the wrath to come.* (1 Thessalonians 1:10)

> *For God hath not appointed us to wrath, but to obtain salvation by our Lord Jesus Christ.* (1 Thessalonians 5:9)

The Natural Man Has No Relationship with God and Nothing to Offer Him

Paul teaches us more about the natural man when he reminds his Christian readers of their condition before they were saved. They were spiritually separated from God:

> *For when ye were the servants of sin, ye were **free from righteousness.*** (Romans 6:20, emphasis added)

And you hath he quickened, *who were **dead in trespasses and sins**; Wherein in time past ye walked according to the course of this world, **according to the prince of the power of the air**, the spirit that now worketh in the children of disobedience: Among whom also we all had our conversation in times past in the lusts of our flesh, **fulfilling the desires of the flesh and of the mind**; and were by nature the children of wrath, even as others.... Even when we were dead in sins, hath quickened us together with Christ, (by grace ye are saved;) ... That at that time ye were without Christ, being aliens from the commonwealth of Israel, and strangers from the covenants of promise, **having no hope, and without God in the world**.* (Ephesians 2:1-3, 5, 12, emphasis added)

*And you, being **dead in your sins** and the uncircumcision of your flesh, hath he quickened together with him, having forgiven you all trespasses.* (Colossians 2:13, emphasis added)

*But God be thanked, that **ye were the servants of sin**, but ye have obeyed from the heart that form of doctrine which was delivered you.* (Romans 6:17, emphasis added)

Paul and the writer of the letter to the Hebrews both remind their readers that before they were saved, nothing they did pleased God or had any eternal value:

But without faith it is impossible to please him: for he that cometh to God must believe that he is, and that he is a rewarder of them that diligently seek him. (Hebrews 11:6)

What fruit had ye then in those things whereof ye are now ashamed? for the end of those things is death. (Romans 6:21)

For when we were in the flesh, the motions of sins, which were by the law, did work in our members to bring forth fruit unto death. (Romans 7:5)

The Natural Man is Darkened in His Mind

As it relates to spirituality, another important characteristic of the natural man is that he is utterly incapable of understanding spiritual truth. This is so because the natural man is spiritually dead; he is separated from God who is the author and teacher of spiritual things.

This I say therefore, and testify in the Lord, that ye henceforth walk not as other Gentiles walk, in the vanity of their mind, Having the understanding darkened, being alienated from the life of God through the ignorance that is in them, because of the blindness of their heart. (Ephesians 4:17-18)

The human spirit is the part of man that knows things. Every person can know things about himself, including the fact that he is an imperfect sinner. Ordinary facts which can be learned and understood by an unsaved person are called "the things of a man." The truths revealed to the church are of a spiritual nature. They can only be understood by one who is spiritually alive, and they can only be taught by the Holy Spirit of God.

For what man knoweth the things of a man, save the spirit of man which is in him? even so the things of God knoweth no man, but the Spirit of God... But the natural man receiveth not the things of

the Spirit of God: for they are foolishness unto him: neither can he know them, because they are spiritually discerned.
(1 Corinthians 2:11, 14)

A natural man becomes spiritually alive when he believes the Gospel of Christ. His faith in Christ's payment for his sins allows God to make pure and holy a place in which He can indwell the new believer. To indwell means that God has come to live inside, communing with the believer's human spirit. The one who believes the Gospel is no longer spiritually dead, meaning separated from God, but is now spiritually alive. This is so because of the union he now has with God who is the source of spiritual life. This condition is the spiritual birth known also as "born again," "regenerated," or "born from above."

The Holy Spirit who now indwells the believer can teach him spiritual truth. This is known as the illuminating ministry of the Holy Spirit. A natural man has not had a spiritual birth, does not have the indwelling Holy Spirit, and therefore cannot know the spiritual things of God. When he considers spiritual truth, he finds it foolish.

For the preaching of the cross is to them that perish foolishness; but unto us which are saved it is the power of God.
(1 Corinthians 1:18)

The Natural Man is an Enemy of God

The natural man is an enemy of God, whether or not he intends to be so. He is part of Satan's world system which is opposed to the plan of God. No matter how good it seems to be, in its philosophy, in its quality, and in its method, Satan's world system does not meet God's standards. Everyone in it is operating in competition with the plan of God and in violation of scripture.

> *For if, when we were enemies, we were reconciled to God by the death of his Son, much more, being reconciled, we shall be saved by his life.* (Romans 5:10)

> *And you, that were sometime alienated and enemies in your mind by wicked works, yet now hath he reconciled.* (Colossians 1:21)

If a natural man denies that he is an enemy or a sinner, he is calling God a liar. Because he cannot walk by faith, he can only produce things that are of a sinful quality. He can only operate under the dominion of sin and by the principles of Satan's world system. No matter how good his deeds appear, the product of the natural man is not acceptable to God. One of Satan's many abilities is the creation of convincing counterfeits. His children can do kind, generous, helpful and even sacrificial things. What they cannot do is understand God or the way in which His program operates. A natural man may not be a wicked man by the world's estimation, but the most he can achieve is to be outwardly moral by the power of his own sinful flesh, to the best of his own ability and willpower. Not one good deed he does will undo the sins he has committed against God. He is guilty of his sins regardless of his admirable actions. He is a slave to sin, blind to the truth, and he cannot be saved from eternal fire without believing the Gospel of Christ. By his rejection of the truth, he has chosen his enemy status and his eternal separation from God.

A Christian, however, is saved: he is delivered from the enslaving power of sin and has been transferred from the authority and jurisdiction of darkness. The Christian has been born into the family of God, and he can never be "un-born." He has been sealed with the Holy Spirit Himself, *"unto the day of redemption."* (Ephesians 4:30) He will never again be a natural man.

For He rescued us from the domain of darkness, and transferred us to the kingdom of His beloved Son. (Colossians 1:13, NASB)

Chapter 2

THE SPIRITUAL MAN

The study of spirituality includes three spiritual conditions described in the Bible. These three conditions are represented by three kinds of men: the natural man, the spiritual man, and the carnal man. The natural man is an unsaved man. He is spiritually dead because he is separated from God by sin and is, therefore, incapable of producing spiritual fruit. The two other kinds of men, the spiritual man and the carnal man, are both saved, but each is operating by a different source of inspiration and power for living. Only the fruit of the spiritual man is pleasing to God and brings Him glory.

What is a Spiritual Man?

A spiritual man is one who emanates the things of the Spirit of God, displaying God's character in his words and actions. His spiritual capabilities are accessed by counting what God says to be true, and by placing his faith in God's promises. His motives are pure and his choices are holy. He is walking in freedom from both the power of sin within him and the influence of Satan and his world system. He is filled with all that the Holy Spirit has to give him, including spiritual understanding and enabling power.

The spiritual man is both a man within whom God lives and one who is acting in cooperation with God. Because he has believed the Gospel of Christ, 1 Corinthians 15:1-4, he is no longer dead in trespasses and sins, meaning separated from God by sin. His human spirit has been washed by spiritual regeneration, making it a holy dwelling place for God.

> *Not by works of righteousness which we have done, but according to his mercy he saved us, by the washing of regeneration, and renewing of the Holy Ghost.* (Titus 3:5)

God's indwelling presence is what makes a Christian spiritually alive (also known as born again), because God is the source of spiritual life. The human spirit is one component of the non-physical part of man, called the mind; the soul is the other component.

> *And the very God of peace sanctify you wholly; and* I pray God *your whole spirit and soul and body be preserved blameless unto the coming of our Lord Jesus Christ.* (1 Thessalonians 5:23)

The members of the Godhead are literally connected to the believer, communing in the spirit part of his mind. Before salvation, every person lives in darkness, ignorance, and rebellion, whether or not he intends to. Upon being born again, the new Christian is provided with the mind of Christ; this means he has access to God's wisdom and can learn the truths of scripture.

> *This I say therefore, and testify in the Lord, that ye henceforth walk not as other Gentiles walk, in the vanity of their mind, Having the understanding darkened, being alienated from the life of God through the ignorance that is in them, because of the blindness of their heart: ... But ye have not so learned Christ; If so be that ye have heard him, and have been taught by him, as the truth is in Jesus.* (Ephesians 4:17-18, 20-21)

For who hath known the mind of the Lord, that he may instruct him? But we have the mind of Christ. (1 Corinthians 2:16)

If any of you lack wisdom, let him ask of God, that giveth to all men liberally, and upbraideth not; and it shall be given him. (James 1:5)

The spiritual man does not have the omniscience of God, but he can understand what God wants him to know and he is able to use what he learns. If he counts himself to be what God says that he is and lives accordingly, by faith, he remains spiritual.

The Spiritual Man is Spiritually Illuminated and Can Know the Things of God

In order to live in accordance with God's will, the spiritual man must understand who God has made him, what God expects of him, and by what method he is to operate. He is no longer to live according to the principles of Satan's world system, nor by the relative morality of his own opinions. If the spiritual man so desires, the Holy Spirit will provide him with spiritual illumination to know the "deep things of God." These truths, found in the letters to the church, were given to its members, the body of Christ. The spiritual man can understand and apply these teachings to his life.

According to scripture, the spirit part of the human mind is the part that knows things, and only a regenerated mind can know spiritual things:

But as it is written, Eye hath not seen, nor ear heard, neither have entered into the heart of man, the things which God hath prepared *for them that love him. But **God hath revealed them unto us by his Spirit:** for the Spirit searcheth all things, yea, **the deep things of God**. For what man knoweth the things of a man, save the spirit of man which is in him? even so the things of God knoweth no man, but the Spirit of God. Now we have received, not the spirit of the world, but the spirit which is of God; **that we might know the things that are freely given to us of God**. Which things also we speak, not in the words which man's wisdom teacheth, but **which the Holy Ghost teacheth**; comparing spiritual things with spiritual. But the natural man receiveth not the things of the Spirit of God: for they are foolishness unto him: neither can he know them, because they are spiritually discerned. But he that is spiritual judgeth all things, yet he himself is judged of no man. For who hath known the mind of the Lord, that he may instruct him? But **we have the mind of Christ**.* (1 Corinthians 2:9-16, emphasis added)

The Spiritual Man Can Spiritually Mature

In addition to knowing God, the spiritual man is able to see himself more clearly. His self-awareness started at his initial salvation when he recognized himself as a sinner with no righteousness to qualify him for heaven. As he grows in his knowledge of scripture, the Holy Spirit reveals to him the areas of his life which are not in accordance with God's will. His agreement with God allows him to be Spirit-filled. The increasing consistency of spirituality is known as Christian maturity.

Furthermore then we beseech you, brethren, and exhort you by the Lord Jesus, that as ye have received of us how ye ought to walk and to please God, so ye would abound more and more. (1 Thessalonians 4:1)

The spiritual man matures as he says, "Yes," to what he learns in scripture and uses it. He begins to change his mind about things, seeing them from God's point of view. His opinions increasingly align with God's. The Holy Spirit actively teaches the spiritual man, showing him the differences between his ideas and God's. The spiritual man is not perfect; his fruitfulness can be mis-directed. The spiritual man's rate of maturity is dependent upon his willingness to learn the scriptures, believe them and cooperate with God in their proper use.

Let us therefore, as many as be perfect, be thus minded: and if in any thing ye be otherwise minded, God shall reveal even this unto you. (Philippians 3:15)

For the grace of God that bringeth salvation hath appeared to all men, Teaching us that, denying ungodliness and worldly lusts, we should live soberly, righteously, and godly, in this present world. (Titus 2:11-12)

To see the truth is to see things as they really are. Only God can always see the truth, but the maturing spiritual man will increasingly see the truth of many things. An example of this can be seen in the life of Paul, who increased in his awareness and abhorrence of his own sin. Living blamelessly before the law, Paul became aware of his sin upon his faith in Jesus Christ as his savior. As he matured, he increasingly saw himself as God did. After his salvation, Paul firstly considered himself the least of apostles:

For I am the least of the apostles, that am not meet to be called an apostle, because I persecuted the church of God. (1 Corinthians 15:9)

As Paul progressed in maturity, so humbled was he that he considered himself to be at the bottom of a much larger group; he considered himself the least of saints:

> *Unto me, who am less than the least of all saints, is this grace given, that I should preach among the Gentiles the unsearchable riches of Christ.* (Ephesians 3:8)

At the end of his ministry, Paul, to whom the risen Christ had personally delivered the doctrines of Christianity, was so aware of his own failings and sinfulness that he branded himself the chief of sinners:

> *This is a faithful saying, and worthy of all acceptation, that Christ Jesus came into the world to save sinners; of whom I am chief.* (1 Timothy 1:15)

With spiritual maturity comes more reality, including greater appreciation of one's salvation. As the spiritual man increasingly recognizes the worthlessness of the things of the world, and the wretchedness of himself, God's boundless mercy and unfathomable love shine all the more brightly.

The Spiritual Man Adjusts Himself to God

The spiritual man maintains his spirituality by keeping his mind in agreement with God's viewpoint. He communes with God in the spirit of his mind and allows God to continue to teach him what is right, good and acceptable. The Spirit of God compares the spiritual man's attitude and conduct to the spiritual words of scripture to enable him to recognize and discern his condition and in so doing make any adjustments needed to remain spiritual.

Which things also we speak, not in the words which man's wisdom teacheth, but which the Holy Ghost teacheth; comparing spiritual things with spiritual. (1 Corinthians 2:13)

As he continues to learn and keeps in mind the teachings of scripture, the spiritual man recognizes when he has diverted from God's path. God Himself reveals the discrepancy so that the fellowship between them may remain unbroken. The spiritual man examines himself, allowing the Holy Spirit to search his thoughts and motives.

For if we would judge ourselves, we should not be judged. But when we are judged, we are chastened of the Lord, that we should not be condemned with the world. (1 Corinthians 11:31-32)

For though he was crucified through weakness, yet he liveth by the power of God. For we also are weak in him, but we shall live with him by the power of God toward you. Examine yourselves, whether ye be in the faith; prove your own selves. Know ye not your own selves, how that Jesus Christ is in you, except ye be reprobates? (2 Corinthians 13:4-5)

When his conscience warns him regarding not acting rightly, the spiritual man says, "Yes," to the witness of his conscience and reverses course. Because of his agreement with God's word and his return to being rightly adjusted to the Spirit, he remains spiritual rather than sinning. His spirituality is maintained because he counts it to be true that he need not sin. He continues to depend upon the power of God and the freedom provided by his salvation from sin.

> *For if we have been planted* (i.e. buried) *together in the likeness of his death, we shall be also* in the likeness *of his resurrection: Knowing this, that our old man is crucified with* him, *that the body of sin might be destroyed, that* **henceforth we should not serve sin. For he that is dead is freed from sin.** *(*Romans 6:5-7, synonym and emphasis added)

The Spiritual Man Protects His Mind

The spiritual man proactively protects himself from what the Bible calls the carnal mind. The carnal or fleshly mind refers to the condition of thinking like an unsaved person rather than a saved person. Carnal thinking leads to sin.

> *For they that are after the flesh do mind the things of the flesh; but they that are after the Spirit the things of the Spirit. For to be carnally minded is death; but to be spiritually minded is life and peace. Because the carnal mind is enmity against God: for it is not subject to the law of God, neither indeed can be.* (Romans 8:5-7)

The mind of the spiritual man is an unruffled mind. He is not thrown off course by false teaching, nor overwrought by displeasing circumstances. He does not allow his testimony to be damaged with his reactions to unexpected events. He does not become agitated in his thinking, allowing his thoughts to race or to get stuck when life is not going his way. He keeps in mind his knowledge of God's provision for him so that he does not return to the way of thinking and behaving that characterized him as a natural man. The spiritual man experiences and retains a peaceful mind by faith.

Now the God of hope fill you with all joy and peace in believing,
that ye may abound in hope, through the power of the Holy Ghost.
(Romans 15:13)

And the peace of God, which surpasses all comprehension,
will guard your hearts and your minds in Christ Jesus.
(Philippians 4:7 NASB)

Because the principle of sin still operates within the spiritual man, and because he is bombarded continually with ungodly and Satanically inspired messages, the spiritual man protects himself by renewing his mind with the truth of God's word. He knows that God provides him with both the desire and the ability to continue to learn and implement scripture so that he will not be deceived if presented with false doctrine.

That we henceforth be no more children, tossed to and fro,
and carried about with every wind of doctrine, by the sleight of
men, and cunning craftiness, whereby they lie in wait to deceive.
(Ephesians 4:14)

And be not conformed to this world: but be ye transformed by the
renewing of your mind, that ye may prove what is that good, and
acceptable, and perfect, will of God. (Romans 12:2)

And be renewed in the spirit of your mind. (Ephesians 4:23)

For it is God which worketh in you both to will and to do of his
good pleasure. (Philippians 2:13)

Set your mind on the things above, not on the things that are on earth. (Colossians 3:2 NASB)

By setting his mind on things above, the spiritual man is not ignoring his earthly responsibilities or living in a fantasy. He is placing a mental "picture frame" around his thoughts and not allowing himself to spend time reflecting on ungodly things, or on things that will rob him of his peace and faith in God. He is actively limiting his mind in order to protect it from things that could lead him away from total reliance upon the Holy Spirit. He does not allow himself to be exposed to things which could deceive him, damage his attitude, or tempt him with ungodly motives or choices.

For our boasting is this: the testimony of our conscience that we conducted ourselves in the world in simplicity and godly sincerity, not with fleshly wisdom but by the grace of God...
(2 Corinthians 1:12a NKJV)

Let no one cheat you of your reward, taking delight in false humility and worship of angels, intruding into those things which he has not seen, vainly puffed up by his fleshly mind.
(Colossians 2:18 NKJV)

Dearly beloved, I beseech you as strangers and pilgrims, abstain from fleshly lusts, which war against the soul... (1 Peter 2:11)

But every man is tempted, when he is drawn away of his own lust, and enticed. Then when lust hath conceived, it bringeth forth sin: and sin, when it is finished, bringeth forth death. Do not err, my beloved brethren. (James 1:14-16)

The illuminating ministry of the Holy Spirit enables the spiritual man to utilize the mind of Christ. This means that he can understand spiritual truth, apply it to his life, and recognize when he has departed from it. He can know the deep things of God which have been revealed only to the church. He has intimate communion with each member of the Godhead, allowing God's ministry within him to flow freely as he is rightly adjusted in attitude, motive and belief. He protects his mind from lying influences and temptations. He rests in God's provision for him in all things. The spiritual man is not necessarily trying to **do** things for God; his focus is on getting to **know** God through His written word, the Bible. As he knows more and uses it, he is more consistently spiritual. He bears spiritual fruit at work, at home, and in Christian service. His spirit-filled condition reflects the character of God in **all that he does**, all to God's glory.

> *But you are a chosen race, a royal priesthood, a holy nation, a people of his own, so that you may proclaim the virtues of the one who called you out of darkness into his marvelous light.*
> (1 Peter 2:9 NET Bible)

Chapter 3

THE CARNAL MAN

In regard to one's spiritual condition, the Bible tells us that there are three kinds of men. A natural man is an unsaved man. He is not capable of understanding spiritual truth or producing any spiritual fruit until he is saved by faith in the Gospel of Christ, 1 Corinthians 15:1-4. If he becomes saved, his condition changes to that of a spiritual man, able to know the deep spiritual things of God and to please God in even the mundane things that he does. Only a spiritual man can operate by faith, produce God's character and mature in his Christian life. If he does not mature, he will return to operating as if he is a natural man even though he is saved. To do so is to be carnal, a reference to his sin-tainted body as the source of all that he does. The life of a carnal man is barren, no matter how many good things he appears to be doing.

> *...but I see a different law in the members of my body, waging war against the law of my mind and making me a prisoner of the law of sin which is in my members. Wretched man that I am! Who will set me free from the body of this death?*
> (Romans 7:23-24 NASB)

What is a Carnal Man?

A carnal man is one who is operating by the power of his flesh. Paul coined the usage of the term "flesh" to mean the human body operating under the control of the sin principle which resides within. The power of grace through faith is the way provided by God to enable a spiritual man to walk free from the dominion of his spiritual enemies. The carnal man is capable of being spiritual, but he is not looking to the promises of God with faith and is therefore not able to access the power of God's grace. Instead, he is operating "in the flesh," and is therefore emanating the things of his flesh, not the things of the Spirit. In the Corinthian church, for example, some members were living "as men," meaning natural men.

> *For ye are yet carnal: for whereas* there is *among you envying, and strife, and divisions, are ye not carnal, and walk as men?* (1 Corinthians 3:3)

> *For when we were in the flesh, the motions of sins, which were by the law, did work in our members to bring forth fruit unto death.* (Romans 7:5)

The condition in which a Christian has allowed the sin principle to regain dominion over his life is known as "fleshliness," or "carnality." Although not visible in English, Paul also calls it "soulishness," because the carnal man is responding to the willful desires of his own soul, rather than to the godly desires of his human spirit, the part of his mind in which God has taken residence.

> *And I, brethren, could not speak unto you as unto spiritual, but as unto carnal, even as unto babes in Christ. I have fed you with milk, and not with meat: for hitherto ye were not able to bear it, neither yet now are ye able. For ye are yet carnal: for whereas there is among you envying, and strife, and divisions, are ye not*

carnal, and walk as men? For while one saith, I am of Paul; and another, I am of Apollos; are ye not carnal? (1 Corinthians 3:1-4)

Because the carnal man is not utilizing the power of God's grace, he is living as if he is unsaved, even if only momentarily. Carnality can last for a minute or it can last for years. The carnal man may continue to attend church, read his Bible, witness and serve, but it is of no consequence to God. Only the works produced by the Holy Spirit within a man are acceptable, pleasing and righteous.

Carnality begins in the mind but eventually manifests itself outwardly. The movement from being carnally minded to producing the works of the flesh is evident and visible. It can be detected in attitude, words and actions. Paul's description of the works of the flesh is not exhaustive; it ends with "and such like," to warn readers that there are an endless number of ways in which the flesh can manifest carnality:

Now the works of the flesh are manifest, which are these; *Adultery, fornication, uncleanness, lasciviousness, Idolatry, witchcraft, hatred, variance, emulations, wrath, strife, seditions, heresies, Envyings, murders, drunkenness, revellings, and such like: of the which I tell you before, as I have also told* you *in time past, that they which do such things shall not inherit the kingdom of God.* (Galatians 5:19-21)

Two Choices: By Faith or by Sin

... for whatsoever is not of faith is sin. (Romans 14:23b)

The Bible teaches that whatever is not of faith is sin. This is a literal truth; whatever a Christian does is produced by one of only two sources: his flesh or the Spirit of God. Whatever is not produced by the power of grace is not of the faith system and is produced by the only other alternative: the flesh. A fleshly product is of a quality of sin, even if it is not what one might consider evil. A Christian can do a "good deed" and God will count it sin if it is produced by the flesh.

At any given moment, a Christian is either carnal and operating in the flesh or he is spiritual and operating in the Spirit. There is no third mode of spiritual operation. When a Christian is operating in cooperation with the Holy Spirit, he is spiritual. He is rightly adjusted to the Spirit and is emanating the things of the Spirit. When he follows the cravings of his flesh or the desires of his soul which are contrary to godliness, he is carnal and is emanating the characteristics and quality of the flesh. There is no in-between or admixture. He is either obeying one master or the other.

> *Know ye not, that to whom ye yield yourselves servants to obey, his servants ye are to whom ye obey; whether of sin unto death, or of obedience unto righteousness?* (Romans 6:16)

> *I speak after the manner of men because of the infirmity of your flesh: for as ye have yielded your members servants to uncleanness and to iniquity unto iniquity; even so now yield your members servants to righteousness unto holiness.* (Romans 6:19)

The Development of Carnality

The state of carnality begins with the mind. A Christian who places restrictions on his mind and does not let it wander into unclean thoughts, self-pity, complaints, self-righteous judgments, pridefulness, worries, and similar things, has the ability to maintain his spirituality. The Christian who allows his mind to dwell upon things such as memories that rob him of his peace, people he does not like, unrighteous ideas, or unhappy circumstances, for example, is setting himself against God.

> *For they that are after the flesh do mind the things of the flesh; but they that are after the Spirit the things of the Spirit. For to be carnally minded is death; but to be spiritually minded is life and peace. Because the carnal mind is enmity against God: for it is not subject to the law of God, neither indeed can be. So then they that are in the flesh cannot please God.* (Romans 8:5-8)

Thoughts lead to words and deeds. The carnally-minded Christian will quickly move to carnality in practice and commit sin. When he is carnal, he is giving over his body as a servant to sin, whether it be his tongue to speak or another member of his body to some kind of unrighteousness. He is not emanating the righteous character of God nor the virtues of Jesus Christ, both of which are produced by the Holy Spirit.

One who is born of the Spirit of God is saved; he is delivered from the penalty for sin and he is also delivered from the domination of the sin principle operating within him. He is able to access the power of grace in order to operate in a Christlike manner. He is no longer a slave to sin:

> *Knowing this, that our old man is crucified with* him, *that the body of sin might be destroyed, that henceforth we should not serve sin. For he that is dead is freed from sin. ... For sin shall not have dominion over you: for ye are not under the law, but under grace.* (Romans 6:6-7, 14)

Living in cooperation with God is a choice. The carnal man has allowed himself to return to operating under the power of sin. He can knowingly choose to sin, or he can slip into sin thoughtlessly if he is not guarding his mind and looking to God's word for wisdom, guidance and power. Something as simple as a nasty remark in a moment of frustration instantly moves the believer into the realm of the flesh.

The body itself is a source of temptation to sin. Its natural cravings were given by God to sustain humanity as a race, to lead men to nourish, protect and replicate themselves. The law of sin within man twists these desires in order to use them for selfish endeavors. The human soul, which can function in accordance with either salvation or sin, is the seat of emotion and volition. It often yearns for things which are contrary to God's will. Satan can add to the temptation of the body or soul by sending his demons to plant ideas, or to offer the enticements and distractions of the world. Peter refers to this internal dynamic as the flesh at war against the soul. This means that the principle of sin within the body tempts the will of man to follow the flesh rather than the Spirit.

> *Dearly beloved, I beseech* you *as strangers and pilgrims, abstain from fleshly lusts which war against the soul.* (1 Peter 2:11)

Chapter 1 of the letter from James details the mental process which leads to sin:

> *Let no man say when he is tempted, I am tempted of God: for God cannot be tempted with evil, neither tempteth he any man: But every man is tempted, when he is drawn away of his own lust,*

and enticed. Then when lust hath conceived, it bringeth forth sin:
and sin, when it is finished, bringeth forth death. (James 1:13-15)

When a temptation presents itself, a Christian is to direct his faith toward the liberating truths of God's word, telling himself that he is dead to sin and that he does not have to yield to the enticement. If he does not, he will consider the temptation a possibility. If he does not repent by rejecting his consideration of the temptation, he will take mental ownership of the sin and act upon it. When he decides to follow through, his desire, or lust, gives birth to sin. When sin occurs, it also has a product: death. He is now a carnal man and has functionally separated himself from God.

The Source of Carnality

The source of carnality is within each person; it is the principle of sin, often called the sin nature. Paul calls it the "law of sin," meaning that it is a way of functioning, similarly to how obeying a traffic law is a way of functioning in traffic. The drive of the sin principle is toward independence, while spirituality requires total reliance upon God. Initial salvation is a renovation of the human spirit, but the human body has not changed and will not change until the resurrection of the saints. At that time all believers will have new bodies in which no sin principle exists. Paul tells us that the sin principle, or "law of sin," resides in our members, meaning our body parts.

For when we were in the flesh, the motions of sins, which were by
*the law, did work **in our members** to bring forth fruit unto death.*
... For I know that in me (that is, in my flesh,) dwelleth no good
thing... (Romans 7:5, 18a, emphasis added)

> *But I see another law in my members, warring against the law of*
> *my mind, and bringing me into captivity to the **law of sin which***
> ***is in my members**... I thank God through Jesus Christ our Lord.*
> *So then with the mind I myself serve the law of God; but with the*
> *flesh the law of sin.* (Romans 7:23, 25, emphasis added)

Paul explained in Romans 7 that his body was working in opposition to the way in which his mind (soul and spirit) was supposed to operate. This is probably the most common reason for carnality. Often it is Satan who is blamed when a Christian sins. Although Satan and his world system can tempt the Christian, they cannot make him do anything. Everyone who has been spiritually born has been freed from the power of sin by the death, burial and resurrection of Jesus Christ. Sins cannot be blamed on Satan.

> *What shall we say then? Shall we continue in sin, that grace may*
> *abound? God forbid. How shall we, that are dead to sin, live any*
> *longer therein? Know ye not, that so many of us as were baptized*
> *into Jesus Christ were baptized into his death? Therefore we are*
> *buried with him by baptism into death: that like as Christ was*
> *raised up from the dead by the glory of the Father, even so we*
> *also should walk in newness of life. For if we have been planted*
> *together in the likeness of his death, we shall be also in the*
> *likeness of his resurrection: Knowing this, that our old man is*
> *crucified with him, that the body of sin might be destroyed, that*
> *henceforth we should not serve sin. For he that is dead is freed*
> *from sin.* (Romans 6:1-7)

The Result of Carnality

This law of sin, or "sin principle" operates in every person, and in a Christian it leads to spiritual "death." When a Christian sins, he acts independently from God. It is as if he is still separated from God, dead in trespasses and sins just as he was before he was saved. This is why Paul calls the sin principle "the law of sin and death." It is a way of functioning that is sinful and causes temporary spiritual death. God still indwells the Christian's spirit; he remains sealed unto the day of redemption. In practice, however, the carnal Christian has returned to living like a natural man. He is grieving the Spirit and doing what He hates.

Spirituality and carnality are matters of faith. When a Christian believes God and exercises faith in His promises, all that he does is spiritual. He can do the mundane tasks of daily life with thanksgiving in his heart and in doing so bring glory to God. If he instead responds to circumstances, other people, or deception from his flesh or a demonic source, then he is not walking by faith and is not depending upon the grace of God to produce spiritual fruit. This functional separation between God and the believer that the Bible calls "death" is commonly referred to as being out of fellowship. Fellowship is partnership; the carnal man is not operating in partnership with God.

> *Let him know, that he which converteth the sinner from the error of his way shall save a soul from death, and shall hide a multitude of sins.* (James 5:20)

Avoiding Carnality

To avoid carnality, a Christian must know that he is in control of his own mind. No person born of the Spirit of God can rightly say, "This is just how I am," or blame his upbringing, situation or other people for his conduct. A Christian can limit his thoughts and control his behavior for he does not do it alone. The righteous Spirit of Almighty God indwells every true believer. His power is always available and always effective. In order to be fruitful, a Christian must trust God's provision for control of his thoughts, actions and tongue.

The Holy Spirit continually ministers His will to the Christian's human spirit, calling his conscience to godliness (the conscience being a function of the mind). The resulting purity of mind is known as having a good conscience toward God. The spiritual man uses the testimony of his conscience and his experience of fruitfulness (joy, peace, self-control, et cetera) as spiritual "feedback" which allows him to discern his spiritual condition so that persistent carnality is avoided.

And herein do I exercise myself, to have always a conscience void of offence toward God, and toward men. (Acts 24:16)

Now the end of the commandment is charity out of a pure heart, and of a good conscience, and of faith unfeigned. (1 Timothy 1:5)

Holding faith, and a good conscience; which some having put away concerning faith have made shipwreck. (1 Timothy 1: 19)

Pray for us: for we trust we have a good conscience, in all things willing to live honestly. (Hebrews 13:18)

Having a good conscience; that, whereas they speak evil of you, as of evildoers, they may be ashamed that falsely accuse your good conversation in Christ. (1 Peter 3:16)

But the fruit of the Spirit is love, joy, peace, longsuffering, gentleness, goodness, faith, Meekness, temperance: against such there is no law. (Galatians 5:22-23)

Christian maturity refers to the increase in consistency of a Christian walking as a spiritual man and less frequently as a carnal man. With maturity, carnal thoughts are more rapidly dismissed, and the circumstances which tend to promote carnality can be recognized before they lead to sin. Maturity is a result of spending time in God's word, believing it, and using it. As a Christian becomes more consistent in using the mind of Christ and making godly choices, his conscience is adjusted, making him more sensitive to wrong-doing and convincing him to reverse course rather than to sin. When a Christian learns to recognize carnality within himself, he can instead choose to yield to righteousness.

Even if a Christian has begun contemplating sin, or has allowed a bad attitude or motive to take hold, this can be reversed by a change of mind. He needs only to redirect his faith to the promises of God, believing that he is able to walk free from sin. In doing so, he is shifting from operating soulishly, according to his desires, and returning to what his spirit knows to be true. It is God's word, engrafted to renew the mind, which reverses the desires of the soul, realigning it with the Spirit of God.

Wherefore lay apart all filthiness and superfluity of naughtiness, and receive with meekness the engrafted word, which is able to save your souls. (James 1:21)

Renewing one's mind with the truth will deliver (save) the soul which has been deceived by the allure of sin. Remaining in ignorance, failing to engage his mind to recognize what is happening around him, or passively allowing his life to follow a fleshly course are snares that can be avoided. To do so, the spiritual man must learn to recognize his own weaknesses and Satan's methods so that he can apply the solutions that God has provided. He must decide if he wishes to intentionally live in such a way that he is informed and empowered by God's word, so that he bears fruit and brings glory to God.

> *Lest Satan should get an advantage of us: for we are not ignorant of his devices.* (2 Corinthians 2:11)

A Note About Law

Not all carnality is the result of rebellion against God, slackness in Christian living, or ungodly desires. Paul's battle with carnality resulted from his enthusiastic efforts to improve his Christian life by adding law. Having been a good Pharisee in his past, he apparently thought that adding some laws might make his Christian walk even better. It must have seemed like a good idea; after all, he described himself as "blameless" in regard to living under the Law of Moses (Philippians 3:6). Paul's blamelessness does not mean that he never sinned. It means that when he did sin, he brought the sacrifice required by law to the temple.

Paul miscalculated by thinking that he could do good by any means other than through the grace of God. The church lives under a different administration than did Israel. We are administered by the internal power of grace through faith, not by external laws.

Perhaps in a moment of self-righteousness, what Paul had forgotten was that the strength of sin is the law. We can see this principle demonstrated by saying to someone, "Don't look behind you!" Invariably, the person who hears this command will either look or be tempted to. The command not to look immediately ignites the sin principle's rebellious desires. This principle is true for any law or set of laws: it tempts one to disobey; it makes disobedience seem desirable. Paul gives the example that as soon as he told himself He should not covet, he instantly felt covetous, causing an inner battle:

> What shall we say then? Is the Law sin? May it never be! On the contrary, I would not have come to know sin except through the Law; for I would not have known about coveting if the Law had not said, "YOU SHALL NOT COVET." But sin, taking opportunity through the commandment, produced in me coveting of every kind; for apart from the Law sin is dead. I was once alive apart from the Law; but when the commandment came, sin became alive and I died; and this commandment, which was to result in life, proved to result in death for me; for sin, taking an opportunity through the commandment, deceived me and through it killed me. (Romans 7:7-11 NASB)

> The sting of death is sin; and the strength of sin is the law. (1 Corinthians 15:56)

When Paul tried to add law to his spiritual life in grace, he was no longer walking by faith. Rather than simply believing God's promises and counting what God says to be true, he looked to an external rule, a "don't." He shifted his faith from the sufficiency of God's grace to the Law. Effectively he was once again spiritually dead, and therefore he was left with only the power of his own sinful flesh to help him to do rightly. This made him the policeman to police himself, and this way of functioning never works. It led Paul immediately into the tug of war described in Romans 7, in which he found himself doing things that he did not want to do. "How to perform" was what was missing; Paul no longer had the ability not to sin and found himself once again captive to the sin principle within him. By functioning in his flesh he returned to being a slave to sin, on the opposing side from God, and in a mental battle with himself. Paul was carnal.

> *For I know that in me (that is, in my flesh,) dwelleth no good thing: for to will is present with me; but* how *to perform that which is good I find not.* (Romans 7:18)

The carnal man has not lost his salvation. He is sealed by the Holy Spirit unto the day of redemption, but he is not cooperating with God. He has not adjusted himself to the leading of the Spirit, and is instead acting independently. He is not operating by faith and cannot please God until he changes his mind about his sin. The moment that the carnal man repents and agrees with God regarding the cause of his carnality, he can return to spirituality. He is once again cooperating with God and the Holy Spirit can freely do His work within him. Every moment, a Christian is either spiritual or carnal; these are the only two possibilities with regard to the source and quality of what he does. Learning to recognize one's spiritual condition and abide in fellowship with God provides lasting joy, contentment, self-control and peace.

> *If we confess our sins, he is faithful and just to forgive us* our *sins, and to cleanse us from all unrighteousness.* (1 John 1:9)

Chapter 4

LIVING BARREN BY QUENCHING THE SPIRIT

A Christian operates in only one of two conditions: he is either operating by the power of the Holy Spirit and is spiritual, or he is carnal, and operating under the dominion of sin. When he is carnal, he cannot produce the fruit of the Spirit and is spiritually barren rather than fruitful. That which is produced by a spiritual Christian is of a righteous quality and is acceptable to God. That which is produced by a carnal Christian is of a sinful quality, falling short of God's standard; it is as if it had been produced by a natural man. Even if the activities of the spiritual and carnal man appear similar, the work that is produced by the carnal man is not a product of faith and is therefore tainted with sin.

Walk in the Spirit, and ye shall not fulfil the lust of the flesh.
(Galatians 5:16b)

Whatever is not of faith is sin. (Romans 14:23b)

The Bible describes two general ways in which one can be carnal. The first of these is known as "quenching the Spirit," which means to be carnal by **not doing** God's will. God's will for his children and the method by which His will to be done is detailed in the letters to the church. Every Christian is called to operate, or "walk" accordingly:

I therefore, the prisoner of the Lord, beseech you that ye walk worthy of the vocation wherewith ye are called. (Ephesians 4:1)

That ye would walk worthy of God, who hath called you unto his kingdom and glory. (1 Thessalonians 2:12)

Therefore we are buried with him by baptism into death: that like as Christ was raised up from the dead by the glory of the Father, even so we also should walk in newness of life. (Romans 6:4)

If we live in the Spirit, let us also walk in the Spirit. (Galatians 5:25)

For we are his workmanship, created in Christ Jesus unto good works, which God hath before ordained that we should walk in them. (Ephesians 2:10)

The Christian life operates by faith. The faith system is in contrast to the law system, which was an external mechanism, a set of rules, that informed its adherents as to what to do and not do in order to obey God. The faith system is an internal system; when the spiritual man looks to a promise of God and believes it, he is able to access that promise and live accordingly. Faith is the mechanism that accesses God's grace; it enables the spiritual man to do what God asks and in the way that He requires. Christians access initial salvation by faith, and the fruitful Christian lives in the same way.

As ye have therefore received Christ Jesus the Lord, so walk ye in him. (Colossians 2:6)

For we walk by faith, not by sight. (2 Corinthians 5:7)

For therein is the righteousness of God revealed from faith to faith: as it is written, The just shall live by faith. (Romans 1:17)

But that no man is justified by the law in the sight of God, it is evident: for, The just shall live by faith. (Galatians 3:11)

What Does It Mean to Quench the Spirit?

A common usage of the word "quench" is to put out, as in putting out a fire. It can also mean to stop something from being accomplished, as in Ephesians 6, in which the shield of faith keeps Satan's arrows from hitting their mark. The spiritual man quenches the Spirit of God when he resists what God is trying to accomplish: to conform him to the image of Christ.

For whom he did foreknow, he also did predestinate to be conformed to the image of his Son, that he might be the firstborn among many brethren. (Romans 8:29)

Almighty God will accomplish His ultimate purpose, but much fruit-bearing is lost when a Christian does not cooperate. This is why Christians are warned that they may face their day of reward with nothing but ash to offer their Creator, Bridegroom and Savior.

If any man's work shall be burned, he shall suffer loss: but he himself shall be saved; yet so as by fire. (1 Corinthians 3:15)

But that which beareth thorns and briers is rejected, and is nigh unto cursing; whose end is to be burned. But, beloved, we are persuaded better things of you, and things that accompany salvation. (Hebrews 6:8-9a)

Quenching can be passive resistance to the Spirit's leading; examples include not acting on ministry opportunities, not making time for God, His word, or other believers, or failing to avoid things that are detrimental to one's spiritual life. Quenching the Spirit can also be the refusal to operate as part of the body of Christ. Every Christian has a function in the body of Christ; every member of the church is "called."

> *God is faithful, by whom ye were called unto the fellowship of his Son Jesus Christ our Lord.* (1 Corinthians 1:9)

> *And let the peace of God rule in your hearts, to the which also ye are called in one body; and be ye thankful.* (Colossians 3:15)

Christians are called to fellowship as part of the spiritual organism known as the body of Christ. Fellowship is partnership. To support and minister to the spiritual and physical needs of other Christians and to partner with each other in evangelism are its primary purposes. If a Christian, for example, refuses to assemble with believers at church or Bible study, even though there is no law that he must, he cannot function as God intends: as an integral part of a spiritual body. Although he can study on his own, he is less likely to mature without the teaching, experience and wisdom offered by other believers. They too are deprived of his contribution. God calls each Christian to know Him through the study of His word, to pray, to assemble, to evangelize and to help the body of Christ.

> *As we have therefore opportunity, let us do good unto all* men, *especially unto them who are of the household of faith.*
> (Galatians 6:10)

*We are bound to thank God always for you, brethren, as it is
fitting, because your faith grows exceedingly, and the love of
every one of you all abounds toward each other.*
(2 Thessalonians 1:3 NKJV)

Since God wants these things and has told us so in the letters to the
church, a Christian who is not doing these things is quenching the
Holy Spirit. He may not realize that he is doing so; from his perspective
he may think that he is just too busy to make time for "church."
Alternatively, he might believe that he cannot do the things that God
expects. The Bible tells us, however, that God is continually available to
produce both the desire and the ability to do all that He asks. One must
only say, "Yes," to God and believe Him.

*For it is God which worketh in you both to will and to do of his
good pleasure.* (Philippians 2:13)

In 1 Thessalonians 5:19, Paul warns us not to quench the Spirit of
God. Nothing more is said about quenching, but as is often the case in
scripture, reading one more verse provides some explanation:

Quench not the Spirit. Despise not prophesyings.
(1 Thessalonians 5:19-20)

Do Not Despise Prophesyings

The word "despise" can mean to view as contemptible, but it can also
mean to treat something as nothing, of no account, and unimportant.
In practice, to despise God's word would be to fail to make use of it.
Doing so thwarts the Holy Spirit's ability to teach, and therefore to lead
the Christian according to God's will. Not despising the teachings of

scripture is part of what allows the spiritual man to avoid quenching the Spirit of God so that he may bear fruit. Learning and rehearsing the truths of God's word renovates the spirit part of the mind, keeping the spiritual man actively engaged with God and His will. The Holy Spirit brings these truths to mind as needed so that the spiritual man can use them, acting on them by faith.

> *And be not conformed to this world: but be ye transformed by the renewing of your mind, that ye may prove what is that good, and acceptable, and perfect, will of God.* (Romans 12:2)

> *And be renewed in the spirit of your mind.* (Ephesians 4:23)

> *But the Comforter, which is the Holy Ghost, whom the Father will send in my name, he shall teach you all things, and bring all things to your remembrance, whatsoever I have said unto you.* (John 14:26)

The word "prophecy" is commonly used today to refer to teachings about the future, but God's prophets were not merely future-tellers. They communicated whatever message God had, whether it was to warn, to instruct, or to remind of things past. Prophets were God's communicators, and the information they shared was called prophecy. At the time of the writing of Paul's letter, the Bible was not yet complete and God gifted people to teach the early church. The writings of scripture came directly as inspiration from God and are therefore prophecy. The Bible describes itself as "God-breathed;" God inspired every word of it through the writers of the Bible. Using the definition of prophecy which means information communicated from God, all the Bible is prophecy.

All Scripture is God-breathed and is useful for teaching, rebuking,
correcting and training in righteousness so that the servant of
God may be thoroughly equipped for every good work.
(2 Timothy 3:16-17 NIV)

The Holy Spirit of God lives within each Christian, communing with his human spirit. He illuminates the spiritual man to the truth and application of scripture, with few limitations due to age, education or intellectual ability. One who hears or reads a teaching of scripture and says, "No," to it, is despising that teaching. There can be many reasons why a Christian finds himself in the position described by the Bible as "despising prophecy." Some are deceived by Satan. Others cannot believe that they are completely equipped to do all that the letters to the church call upon Christians to do. Some have compromised in regard to a biblical teaching that is disputed by the culture. Referring to Paul's letters, Peter warns that dispensing with some of scripture's teachings is an error that leads to the destruction of a steadfast mind, the requirement for a stable Christian life. He also states the solution: maturity and a better knowledge of the Lord:

As also in all his epistles, speaking in them of these things; in
which are some things hard to be understood, which they that are
unlearned and unstable wrest, as they do also the other scriptures,
unto their own destruction. Ye therefore, beloved, seeing ye know
these things before, beware lest ye also, being led away with the
error of the wicked, fall from your own stedfastness. But grow in
grace, and in the knowledge of our Lord and Saviour Jesus Christ.
To him be glory both now and for ever. Amen. (2 Peter 3:16-18)

Paul knew well that some who believed the Gospel of Christ still found some of Christianity's teachings difficult for them. The pervasive carnality of the Corinthians kept them from understanding anything beyond the very basic doctrines of Christianity. They were carnal, thinking and living as would a natural man:

> *And I, brethren, could not speak unto you as unto spiritual, but as unto carnal,* even *as unto babes in Christ. I have fed you with milk, and not with meat: for hitherto ye were not able* to bear it, *neither yet now are ye able. For ye are yet carnal: for whereas* there is *among you envying, and strife, and divisions, are ye not carnal, and walk as men?* (1 Corinthians 3:1-3)

Whether the problem is faith, deception, or refusal, the solution is the same. The Christian who will not be led by a doctrine he dislikes must spend more time in scripture to gain a balanced view. If he will not repent of his carnal mind, he is placing himself back under the authority of the sin principle. He cannot refuse truth and at the same time become more Christlike. His attitude will quickly lead him to sin. Turning away from truth is an attitude of hostility toward God, even if that is not his intention. A Christian is either spiritual and rightly adjusted to God and His word, or he is carnal and taking the side of sin.

> *Because the carnal mind is enmity against God: for it is not subject to the law of God, neither indeed can be.* (Romans 8:7)

To enjoy fellowship with God and bear fruit, a spiritual man must not despise God's word. He must trust God in everything just as he trusted Him for salvation.

The Bible is Sufficient for Christian Living

One of the teachings of the Bible is that God has communicated to the church everything that its members need to know in order to do His will. Topics the Bible does not address fall under Christian liberty and are to be decided using godly wisdom. Paul described the believer as fully equipped to do God's will and Peter wrote that God's power provides all that is needed for godly living under any circumstances. There is nothing that God did not think of, and nothing that He held back from his precious children. In grace, heaven was emptied for the believer: every person born of the Spirit of God has absolutely everything at his disposal that heaven has to offer. If a Christian does not do God's will, it is not because God did not provide for him to do so.

All scripture is given by inspiration of God, and is profitable for doctrine, for reproof, for correction, for instruction in righteousness: That the man of God may be perfect, throughly furnished unto all good works. (2 Timothy 3:16-17)

According as his divine power hath given unto us all things that pertain unto life and godliness, through the knowledge of him that hath called us to glory and virtue. (2 Peter 1:3)

If a man therefore purge himself from these, he shall be a vessel unto honour, sanctified, and meet for the master's use, and prepared unto every good work. (2 Timothy 2:21)

Now the God of peace, that brought again from the dead our Lord Jesus, that great shepherd of the sheep, through the blood of the everlasting covenant, Make you perfect in every good work to do

his will, working in you that which is wellpleasing in his sight,
through Jesus Christ; to whom be glory for ever and ever. Amen.
(Hebrews 13:20-21)

The preceding verses are the Bible's own testimony to its sufficiency in leading the spiritual man to live consistently within the will of God. Regardless of what is lacking in man, nothing is missing or lacking in scripture. As the Holy Spirit ministers spiritual truth to the human spirit, the spiritual man finds fewer reasons to quench its testimony and leading. He is able to walk out of the darkness of disbelief, fear or deception. Any doubts that he harbors are removed from his mind as the Holy Spirit convinces him of the truth and power of scripture. As he continues to say, "Yes," to God rather than quenching the Spirit by saying, "No," his experience leads him to alter his expectations in favor of God, building his faith and increasing his spiritual maturity.

For God hath not given us the spirit of fear; but of power, and of
love, and of a sound mind. (2 Timothy 1:7)

Help from the Old Testament

If a Christian recognizes that he is quenching the Spirit, the answer is always to go back to God's word. While the letters to the church are the "how-to" of fruitful living, sometimes what is needed is to reacquaint oneself with God Himself. The Old Testament is a priceless treasure trove of what Paul calls the "comfort of the scriptures."

For whatsoever things were written aforetime were written for our
learning, that we through patience and comfort of the scriptures
might have hope. (Romans 15:4)

The nation of Israel lived under the Law of Moses. The Jews were to know its precepts thoroughly and obey them. Their relationship with God was legal, not personal. There was no liberty in which to exercise discernment and nothing to empower obedience. The Old Testament saints had to do the best they could by their own power. Because of this, the Old Testament is full of examples of the Jews' repeated failures, making obvious their need for a savior from sin.

Because of this cycle of failure on the part of the nation, the Old Testament is a showcase of the matchless mercy and grace of God. He is full of compassion, giving them many chances and pitying their wretched state. His incredible patience is on display as Israel fails again and again. Although some of their actions angered God, He never broke His promises nor forsook them. One day He will return to rescue and restore his holy nation. From the descriptions of God's compassionate and longsuffering character, the body of Christ can find comfort and hope, which is the confident expectation that our unchanging God always does rightly, and that all His ways are good.

Additionally, the bountiful blessings of grace when compared to the hard life under law should allay any fears or doubts regarding God's good intention. He does not set up his people to fail, ask them to do what they cannot do, nor leave them without information or help. Under grace, God does not punish his children for non-compliance, nor ask them to find it within themselves to do what He asks. A spiritual man who desires to mature might pray, "Lord, I do not want to quench your work within me. Your word says that you will give me the ability to do these things, and to even want to do them. I know this is true and I will remind myself of it until I believe it without doubting."

A spiritual man lives in cooperation with God and bears spiritual fruit, showing forth the glorious character of God in all that he does. He knows that the church as a whole is called to function as a body, interacting and working together to help and support each other and to evangelize the lost. The spiritual man is aware that the Holy Spirit leads him individually to act upon his calling. In order to avoid quenching the Spirit, he must adjust himself to God's program and increase in his knowledge of God so that he will more consistently and confidently say, "Yes," to Him. The spiritual man's willingness to agree with and rely upon God allows the Spirit to produce within him the desire and ability to do God's will.

Chapter 5

LIVING BARREN BY GRIEVING THE SPIRIT

The Bible describes two broad causes of carnality. The first is quenching the Spirit, which results from a failure to act according to the leading of the Holy Spirit as revealed in scripture. Quenching is carnality by "not doing." The second cause of carnality is called grieving the Spirit. Grieving is carnality by actively doing something contrary to God's word; in other words, it means to commit sin.

> *And grieve not the holy Spirit of God, whereby ye are sealed unto the day of redemption.* (Ephesians 4:30)

One who is born of the Spirit is God's temple; the spirit part of his mind is literally God's dwelling place. Unlike the human body in which the sin principle resides, the spirit of a Christian has been "saved," meaning it has been washed clean and delivered from sin in order to be a holy place for God.

A Christian's spirit exists in communion and agreement with God. This is why a spiritual man desires to do God's will. As he enjoys the benefits resulting from spiritual fruitfulness, the spiritual man values maintaining unbroken fellowship with God; he agrees with God that the joy of fruit-bearing is superior to the temporary pleasures of sin. He sees the deceitfulness of sin, and because of the indwelling Holy Spirit, the desire of his spirit is opposed to the desire of his flesh. If he sins, it creates an internal conflict.

...for the flesh doth desire contrary to the Spirit, and the Spirit contrary to the flesh, and these are opposed one to another, that the things that ye may will—these ye may not do.
(Galatians 5:17, YLT)

For what I am doing, I do not understand; for I am not practicing what I would like to do, but I am doing the very thing I hate. ... For I know that nothing good dwells in me, that is, in my flesh; for the willing is present in me, but the doing of the good is not. For the good that I want, I do not do, but I practice the very evil that I do not want. (Romans 7:15, 18-19 NASB)

The flesh, meaning the body indwelt by the principle of sin, never reforms. It is active in every person, saved or unsaved, until the body is in the grave. Christians, however, are capable of "reckoning" or counting themselves dead to its power. If a spiritual man does not count to be true what God says is true, he will not maintain his freedom from the persistent urges of the flesh. He will grieve the Spirit by returning to sin again and again.

Likewise reckon ye also yourselves to be dead indeed unto sin, but alive unto God through Jesus Christ our Lord. (Romans 6:11)

It's Not Sin; It's My Personality

Some aspects of the sin principle are so ingrained that a Christian may think of them simply as a part of himself, a part of his personality. A Christian might claim to be naturally sarcastic, for example, and deny that his attitude is ungodly. But would he make the sarcastic remark to the face of Jesus Christ? If not, the personality defense may need rethinking.

Christians have the mind of Christ; they are enabled to think and respond as He would and therefore cannot say, "That's just how I am."

Some sins, such as a quick temper, cursing, or making contemptuous sounds are nearly instantaneous reactions. A Christian might believe that to stop before committing such a sin is impossible, as it happens too fast. To be delivered from such sins, he must tell himself that his belief is a lie. He can speak and behave in a godly manner and learn to stop before sinning. He is not the prisoner of his personality, training, environment or culture.

The character of one's flesh might be impatient, dramatic, stingy, covetous, self-important, short-tempered, lazy or indifferent. But Jesus Christ is productive, longsuffering, humble, generous, calm, kind, and the epitome of patience. A spiritual man displays the virtues of his Lord, and he does so by faith, accessing his deliverance from sin, known as salvation.

> *Wherefore, my beloved, as ye have always obeyed, not as in my presence only, but now much more in my absence, work out your own salvation with fear and trembling.* (Philippians 2:12)

What Leads to Sin?

Ultimately, sin is a choice; a Christian can fall into sin at any time and once again think and act like a natural man. Even a Christian who did not intend to sin still chose not to utilize the biblical prescription to avoid it. There are many things that might lead a spiritual man into sin. He might become occupied with an idea, an annoyance, a memory, a physical craving, or something he sees. Satisfaction, contentment or happiness might seem to lie elsewhere and he is tempted to seek those things apart from God. He might have a strong desire for something that he believes he cannot live without or does not want to do without. If he does not dismiss the fleshly idea or walk away from the temptation, he will become carnal and sin.

> *For all that is in the world, the lust of the flesh, and the lust of the eyes, and the pride of life, is not of the Father, but is of the world.* (1 John 2:16)

Temptation to sin is not the true cause of sin, however. The true cause is the failure of a spiritual man to exercise faith in God's promises. A Christian is to live in the same way in which he accessed initial salvation: by faith.

> *As ye have therefore received Christ Jesus the Lord,* so *walk ye in him.* (Colossians 2:6)

> *There hath no temptation taken you but such as is common to man: but God is faithful, who will not suffer you to be tempted above that ye are able; but will with the temptation also make a way to escape, that ye may be able to bear it.* (1 Corinthians 10:13)

Grieving the Spirit Can Be Avoided

The moment when a temptation or sinful habit is recognized, a spiritual man has the ability to direct his faith toward a teaching in God's word that is applicable to the situation. Because he is operating by the power of the Spirit within him, the spiritual man has the ability to refuse to follow through with sin. He may say to himself, "I do not have to do this. I know that I am dead to this temptation and the dead are not tempted. I am free in Christ, and I have the power not to sin. God has provided the strength for me to endure this temptation and walk away." His faith in God's provision immediately energizes the liberating power of God's grace. The spiritual man looks away from the temptation and restricts his mind to the needed truths. In order to do so, he must know these spiritual truths. The spiritual man is consistently in God's word, and as he rehearses what he learns, his reactions change accordingly. He begins to recognize a sinful word before it passes his lips. He knows what triggers his responses and he stops himself. He knows that as a Christian, he has a freedom that no other person has: he is free **not** to sin.

By feeding his spirit with truth instead of feeding the sin-tainted desires of the flesh, the spiritual man will have the awareness and power to maintain his spirituality. Because the world assaults him with a never-ending deluge of error, filth, deception and temptation, the renewing of his mind with truth must also be ongoing.

Finally, brethren, whatsoever things are true, whatsoever things are honest, whatsoever things are just, whatsoever things are pure, whatsoever things are lovely, whatsoever things are of good report; if there be any virtue, and if there be any praise, think on these things. (Philippians 4:8)

Set your mind on the things above, not on the things that are on earth. (Colossians 3:2 NASB)

And be renewed in the spirit of your mind. (Ephesians 4:23)

And be not conformed to this world: but be ye transformed by the renewing of your mind, that ye may prove what is that good, and acceptable, and perfect, will of God. (Romans 12:2)

It is man's own desire, attitude or belief that entices him to sin. Common culprits include injured pride, a sense of entitlement, self pity or exasperation. Such a mindset allows him to nurse his fleshly mind rather than to dismiss ungodly thoughts. In other cases, God is blamed for temptation. Worship, praise and the giving of thanks to God will aid the spiritual man in resisting this lie. God is not testing him; God does not want him to sin.

> *Let no man say when he is tempted, I am tempted of God: for God cannot be tempted with evil, neither tempteth he any man: But every man is tempted, when he is drawn away of his own lust, and enticed.* (James 1:13-14)

Every Christian is equipped to withstand the temptation to sin and to know the truth that protects him from error.

> *For when ye were the servants of sin, ye were free from righteousness. ... But now being made free from sin, and become servants to God, ye have your fruit unto holiness, and the end everlasting life.* (Romans 6:20, 22)

The spiritual man is able to avoid grieving the Spirit because he understands the faith system. Faith must be *in* something; it must have an object. Taking a moment to direct faith toward God's provision and power enables the spiritual man to withstand temptation rather than react according to the sin principle. He recognizes impulses that are contrary to an unruffled state of mind, and stops to think before he speaks in order to avoid dishonoring God. Because he can change his mind before he sins in word or deed, the spiritual man's interactions are calm and reasonable, and do not lead to rash words or choices.

Wherefore, my beloved brethren, let every man be swift to hear,
slow to speak, slow to wrath: For the wrath of man worketh not
the righteousness of God. (James 1:19-20)

Let your moderation be known unto all men. The Lord is at
hand. Be careful for nothing; but in every thing by prayer and
supplication with thanksgiving let your requests be made known
unto God. And the peace of God, which passeth all understanding,
shall keep your hearts and minds through Christ Jesus.
(Philippians 4:5-7)

What If I Have Already Sinned?

A Christian can immediately return to spirituality through repentance, meaning a change of mind, and confession. When he sins, he recognizes it and rapidly acknowledges it to his Father. He comes into agreement with God about the sin rather than justifying it or pursuing it. He finds that he is able to walk free from some of the sins which used to plague him. The spiritual man is not sinless, but the more truth he learns, the more ground he gains against the law of sin.

And ye shall know the truth, and the truth shall make you free.
(John 8:32)

If we confess our sins, he is faithful and just to forgive us our sins,
and to cleanse us from all unrighteousness. (1 John 1:9)

It is worthwhile to note that confession is not simply admitting to sin. The word "confess" means to "say the same thing," which indicates agreement. When we say the same thing about our sin as God says about it, we are in agreement with God. This agreement in regard to sin amounts to a mindset of repentance; it is a change of mind in regard to the sin in question. The changed mind leads to changed behavior.

As soon as the carnal man turns from the sin and returns to dependence upon God, he is spiritual. The move from carnality to spirituality can be as seamless as was the fall from spirituality to sin. When the carnal man becomes aware that he is on the wrong track, he might simply confess to God, "This is no good; I am wrong here." He might have had a change of heart or he might have realized that he acted without giving any thought to God. Sorrow may or may not accompany his repentance. While godly sorrow does lead to repentance (2 Corinthians 7:10), emotional reactions are not a requirement for spirituality.

I Am Saved; Is It Really Such a Big Deal to Sin?

Awake to righteousness, and sin not; for some have not the knowledge of God: I speak this to your shame.
(1 Corinthians 15:34)

Carnality grieves God and exposes him to the filth of sin. Exposing his precious Lord to ugly thoughts, selfish emotions and wasted moments should grieve the Christian as well. To sin is to treat Christ's sacrifice on the cross with an attitude of contempt, indifference, or selfishness. Christ paid for mankind's freedom with His own blood in order to bestow everlasting benefit. God asks His children to use their deliverance from sin for His glory, not to put Christ's work to shame.

Take heed therefore unto yourselves, and to all the flock, over the which the Holy Ghost hath made you overseers, to feed the church of God, which he hath purchased with his own blood. (Acts 20:28)

What? know ye not that your body is the temple of the Holy Ghost
which is in you, which ye have of God, and ye are not your own?
For ye are bought with a price: therefore glorify God in your body,
and in your spirit, which are God's. (1 Corinthians 6:19-20)

Although the spirit and soul of man are non-physical and are therefore
not "members" of the body, they exist in the body, making the body
God's own temple. Because the Christian has been purchased by God
from the slave market of sin, his life is really not his own to waste,
and yet, God allows him a world full of choices every day. One's
earthly lifestyle can devour resources such as time, money, energy,
and motivation. In a world of liberty, holiness is often forgotten. God
does not desire the external holiness created by law and rules, but the
internal holiness resulting from love, the spiritual fruit of God working
through His yielded child.

God desires to conform each Christian to the beautiful, temperate and
peaceful character of His Son. He wants to reward each one richly, even
into eternity, for living for Him here on earth. Paul was so passionate
to become conformed to Christ that he actually considered his earthly
achievements not just a "zero" but a "negative" to his spiritual growth.
He desired gain for Christ's glory, and therefore counted his earthly
gains to be deductions from achieving that goal.

But what things were gain to me, those I counted loss for Christ.
Yea doubtless, and I count all things but loss for the excellency of
the knowledge of Christ Jesus my Lord: for whom I have suffered
the loss of all things, and do count them but dung, that I may win
Christ, And be found in him, not having mine own righteousness,

> *which is of the law, but that which is through the faith of Christ,*
> *the righteousness which is of God by faith.* (Philippians 3:7-9)

Paul considered his relationship with his Savior to be his greatest prize; such a mindset facilitates a Spirit-filled life that can be lived with much freedom from sin and the grief it produces both here and in heaven. Much is lost when a Christian grieves the Spirit with sin. Losses include glory to God, earthly good works and heavenly rewards. One can claim to not care about heavenly rewards, but God Himself arranged for His children to have them; they should not be indifferent to gifts borne out of His love. Why tread upon Christ's sacrifice and deny Him the crowns He wishes for them to lay at His feet? Why deny blessing to others because of one's needless failure to produce? A Christian might say, "Let someone else do it." The Bible does not teach, however, that someone else can do what God intends for him. When Jonah ran from the Lord, the Lord did not find someone else to go to Ninevah. The job was for Jonah. If a Christian does not witness, pray, bless or help, he does not know if what he would have done will get done another way.

> *How then shall they call on him in whom they have not believed?*
> *and how shall they believe in him of whom they have not heard?*
> *and how shall they hear without a preacher?* (Romans 10:14)

A spiritual man can avoid grieving the Spirit of God by firstly recognizing what leads him to sin. Every action comes from a decision. No Christian is the prisoner of his habits or desires, no matter how it feels or appears. A Christian can believe God, bear fruit, honor his precious Savior, and give glory to God.

Chapter 6

THE FILLING OF THE SPIRIT

...be filled with the Spirit. (Ephesians 5:18b)

The spiritual man is filled with the Holy Spirit of God. The state of being filled with the Spirit is a fact of being spiritual. The Spirit's enabling power is flowing freely through the spiritual man so that God can accomplish that which He wills. Being filled is the opposite of quenching and grieving the Spirit. The spiritual man is rightly adjusted to God and is cooperating with God. He is saying, "Yes," to God and is neither quenching the Spirit by refusing the Spirit's leading nor grieving the Spirit by sinning. The spiritual man is looking to the promises of God with faith; he is yielded to God's righteous intention and leading, rather than to the cravings of his flesh. The Christian who is filled is utilizing the enabling power of God's grace:

And he said unto me, My grace is sufficient for thee: for my strength is made perfect in weakness. Most gladly therefore will I rather glory in my infirmities, that the power of Christ may rest upon me. (2 Corinthians 12:9)

Thou therefore, my son, be strong in the grace that is in Christ Jesus. (2 Timothy 2:1)

Let us therefore come boldly unto the throne of grace, that we
may obtain mercy, and find grace to help in time of need.
(Hebrews 4:16)

Wherefore we receiving a kingdom which cannot be moved, let us
have grace, whereby we may serve God acceptably with reverence
and godly fear. (Hebrews 12:28)

The filling of the Spirit is a doctrine that might be misunderstood because it sounds as if we are seeking something from the Holy Spirit. Filling, however, is not accomplished by seeking; it is a state that exists when a believer is yielded to God. The Spirit is free to illuminate, correct and teach the spiritual man and to produce spiritual fruit within him. There is no seeking to be done. All the spiritual blessings that God has to bestow have already been provided to the believer.

Blessed be the God and Father of our Lord Jesus Christ, who hath
blessed us with all spiritual blessings in heavenly places in Christ.
(Ephesians 1:3)

In order to use his spiritual blessings, the spiritual man must know about them and believe them. God asks him to yield the entirety of himself for the purpose of righteousness so that he can be utilized as an effectual member of the body of Christ. The spiritual man whose soul is divided between doing what he knows in his spirit to be right, and what is tempting to his flesh, is unstable. He is not exercising faith and will quickly become carnal.

But let him ask in faith, nothing wavering. For he that wavereth
is like a wave of the sea driven with the wind and tossed. For let

not that man think that he shall receive any thing of the Lord. A double minded man is unstable in all his ways. (James 1:6-8)

Neither yield ye your members as instruments of unrighteousness unto sin: but yield yourselves unto God, as those that are alive from the dead, and your members as instruments of righteousness unto God. (Romans 6:13)

I beseech you therefore, brethren, by the mercies of God, that ye present your bodies a living sacrifice, holy, acceptable unto God, which is your reasonable service. (Romans 12:1)

Two Kinds of Filling

Because a spiritual man is already enabled to do all that God wants him to do, the filling that Paul speaks of is not the kind of filling seen in the early days of the church. The believers of that time spoke in foreign tongues they had not been taught and taught doctrines they had never learned. The Holy Spirit was exercising a measure of mental control over those saints. The fledgling church did not yet know the doctrines of the new grace through faith system. They did not yet have the completed word of God.

The filling of the Spirit for today is a filling up of what is lacking. It is the perfecting of God's work done through a yielded believer who must live in a sin-tainted body. The spiritual man is able to agree with God and yield to His will, but he does not think and act in perfection. God makes up the difference in whatever he does.

Wherefore also we pray always for you, that our God would count you worthy of this calling, and fulfil all the good pleasure of his goodness, and the work of faith with power. (2 Thessalonians 1:11)

Epaphras, who is one of you, a servant of Christ, saluteth you, always labouring fervently for you in prayers, that ye may stand perfect and complete in all the will of God. (Colossians 4:12)

But my God shall supply all your need according to his riches in glory by Christ Jesus. (Philippians 4:19)

For this cause we also, since the day we heard it, do not cease to pray for you, and to desire that ye might be filled with the knowledge of his will in all wisdom and spiritual understanding. (Colossians 1:9)

And ye are complete in him, which is the head of all principality and power. (Colossians 2:10)

Now the God of hope fill you with all joy and peace in believing, that ye may abound in hope, through the power of the Holy Ghost. And I myself also am persuaded of you, my brethren, that ye also are full of goodness, filled with all knowledge, able also to admonish one another. (Romans 15:13-14)

When a spiritual man exercises faith toward God in whatever he is doing, whether mowing the lawn or walking the dog, God counts what he does to be perfectly pure and holy. The Spirit of God works through him, filling up what is lacking, fitting or adjusting him to His needs and making his works acceptable.

As ye have therefore received Christ Jesus the Lord, so walk ye in him. (Colossians 2:6)

For we are glad, when we are weak, and ye are strong: and this also we wish, even *your perfection.* (2 Corinthians 13:9)

The purpose of being filled with the Spirit is to bring God the glory that He deserves for the righteous fruit that He produces.

And this I pray, that your love may abound yet more and more in knowledge and in *all judgment; That ye may approve things that are excellent; that ye may be sincere and without offence till the day of Christ; Being filled with the fruits of righteousness, which are by Jesus Christ, unto the glory and praise of God.* (Philippians 1:9-11)

For this cause I bow my knees unto the Father of our Lord Jesus Christ, Of whom the whole family in heaven and earth is named, That he would grant you, according to the riches of his glory, to be strengthened with might by his Spirit in the inner man; That Christ may dwell in your hearts by faith; that ye, being rooted and grounded in love, May be able to comprehend with all saints what is the breadth, and length, and depth, and height; And to know the love of Christ, which passeth knowledge, that ye might be filled with all the fulness of God. Now unto him that is able to do exceeding abundantly above all that we ask or think, according to the power that worketh in us, Unto him be glory in the church by Christ Jesus throughout all ages, world without end. Amen. (Ephesians 3:14-21)

The life of the spiritual man can be summarized as continually saying, "Yes," to God. God does not crush him with His omniscience of his many shortcomings, but in His kindness shows him gradually and fills up what is lacking. He provides understanding of His will through His word, as well as the areas in which to apply them. The image of a light to a path is helpful; such a light does not show everything, but shows the spiritual man what he needs at the time. As he continues to say, "Yes," to God, he is filled with the Spirit and abides with God, who continues to illuminate, teach, and empower. The spiritual man bears spiritual fruit and works that are pleasing to God. The Spirit-filled believer is not perfect, but God makes up the difference, all to His glory.

Chapter 7

THE CHARACTER OF FRUIT

*But the fruit of the Spirit is love, joy, peace, longsuffering,
gentleness, goodness, faith, Meekness, temperance: against such
there is no law. And they that are Christ's have crucified the flesh
with the affections and lusts.* (Galatians 5:22-24)

Spirituality is the condition under which the fruit of the Spirit is
borne. The spiritual Christian is rightly adjusted to the Spirit in
motive, attitude and method of empowerment, and fruitfulness is the
result. Good works are often confused with fruit, but spiritual fruit is
spiritual, and is of a particular character. Works are activities which are
the result of spirituality. Bearing fruit is not a measure of performance
but of yieldedness. The aim of Christian living is not to try harder to
do more, but to be more consistently spiritual. When Jesus said in John
15:5b, "without me ye can do nothing," He meant it literally. Nothing
done apart from total reliance upon God's grace is approved. God is
not necessarily looking for some great religious work; He expects His
children to live as spiritual men, and in so doing all manner of good
works will result.

In all things shewing thyself a pattern of good works. (Titus 2:7a)

*Who gave himself for us, that he might redeem us from all
iniquity, and purify unto himself a peculiar people, zealous of
good works.* (Titus 2:14)

Following are some aspects of the character of spiritual fruit and the life of faith that leads to fruit-bearing. Initially it does take intentional thought to live as a spiritual man, and there may be some "unlearning" to do. And expect God to do a little pruning; He wants Christians to bear fruit, not just leaves.

> *I am the true vine, and my Father is the husbandman. Every branch in me that beareth not fruit he taketh away: and every branch that beareth fruit, he purgeth it, that it may bring forth more fruit.* (John 15:1-2)

Knowing Before Doing

Spirituality has a particular outcome which is to emanate the character of God, also known as bearing the fruit of the Spirit. A spiritual man knows God's character, and is therefore able to recognize when his own mind has become fleshly. When a spiritual man moves his primary focus from his Lord, he can become distracted by the world, confounded by Satan, or carnal as he views the state of the world around him. Maturing spiritually begins with knowing Him through His word which reveals His will. Knowing must come first in order to produce spiritual fruit rather than to just be busy. The Christian has many things to do, but rather than thinking of good works as an aim in themselves, they are better thought of as the many ways in which spirituality can work itself out in one's salvation.

> *Grace and peace be multiplied unto you through the knowledge of God, and of Jesus our Lord.* (2 Peter 1:2)

For if these things be in you, and abound, they make you that ye shall neither be barren nor unfruitful in the knowledge of our Lord Jesus Christ. (2 Peter 1:8)

But grow in grace, and in the knowledge of our Lord and Saviour Jesus Christ. To him be glory both now and for ever. Amen. (2 Peter 3:18)

Internal, not External

Fruit-bearing has a divine power source; it is not an effort to search the flesh for the energy and desire to obey God. The natural man is accustomed to finding strength within himself. He pushes himself to do things he would rather not, to face challenges, to move through suffering, to hold his tongue, and perhaps even to live another day. A spiritual man, however, recognizes that he does not have to find these things within Himself. He looks to a promise of God in scripture with faith, knowing that his reliance upon God will make it so in his life. The spiritual man reads about contentment, for example, and knows it is true. He does not have to try to make himself feel content or convince himself that he is content when he is not. The spiritual man talks to His Father and says in faith, "I know contentment is part of your fruit. There is something I really want, and it is difficult to believe I can live without it, but I will remind myself of this teaching until I believe. I want your will for me because I know it is best by far. I am willing to be made willing to be content." The spiritual man has liberty to make changes to his life, but he knows that he does not need to change his circumstances to be happy and content. He knows that his external circumstances are not the issue in regard to contentment.

Contentment, like all facets of the fruit of the Spirit is the result of a divine internal operation, accessed by faith.

> *But we have this treasure in earthen vessels, that the excellency of the power may be of God, and not of us.* (2 Corinthians 4:7)

Grace, not Law

Fruit-bearing is gracious, not legal. Law operates in a particular way; the mechanism for its functioning is an external system of rules. Law can be thought of as a fence that is not to be crossed. Law often triggers carnality. The flesh has desires which the law denies, and the denial creates a temptation to break the law. Additionally, law provides no enabling power to obey.

Grace is an internal system that operates by faith; it works when the spiritual man trusts God to do as He has promised. In contrast to an external barrier, the Holy Spirit works within the Christian, leading him to adjust his conscience to God's standards, and bringing to mind God's will as revealed in scripture.

> *All things are lawful unto me, but all things are not expedient: all things are lawful for me, but I will not be brought under the power of any... all things are lawful for me, but all things edify not.* (1 Corinthians 6:12, 10:23b)

The spiritual man must still obey laws, but he does so by the power of grace. For example, the natural man might break the traffic laws to get home faster. The carnal man might outwardly comply, but his mind is in rebellion; he wants to speed home. This kind of obedience does not please God, nor does it fool Him; it is not of a righteous quality.

The spiritual man counts everything that God allows in his life to be good, even slow traffic. In keeping with that attitude, he takes the time in traffic for one of many possibilities which bring God glory. Grace provides the illumination to rightly adjust oneself to God, the will to cooperate with God, and the ability to follow through.

And we have known that to those loving God all things do work together for good. (Romans 8:28a YLT)

"How" Above "What"

Spiritual fruit is of a particular quality. It is produced by a holy God, and has value beyond this life. Even if nobody on earth sees a Christian's good works, his yieldedness brings glory to God. How he does his good works is vastly more important than what works he does. If his works are produced by the power of his flesh, they bring no glory to God. Only in being spiritual can the Christian produce the quality of works that God desires. Works that are worthy are produced by the power of God's grace, accessed by faith. Whatever is not produced by the faith system is of the same quality as sin, because it was produced by the sin-tainted flesh. This is why the "how" of fruit-bearing is vital. The task might be utterly ordinary, like doing the dishes, but it is done with thankfulness that there is food to dirty the dishes, and with faith that performing the task is something that God wills to be done. That mindset makes the work a product of spirituality, and it is therefore pleasing to God.

When a spiritual man does his work without complaining, and without even thinking a complaint because he is filled with spiritual joy and contentment, he brings glory to God. The spiritual man is free from fretting about whether God is pleased with this activity or that one. He knows that he is free to choose how he will serve God and that what he does **will** please God because God is the one who produced the pure motive and grace empowered ability for him to do rightly.

Because the spiritual man operates "how" God wants him to, he has liberty as to "what" he does. He uses his liberty in Christ to make choices about things not addressed in scripture, and he asks God to intervene if he errs. He accesses God's wisdom to avoid foolish or harmful things, and rests in the knowledge that he is a mature son of the Father, free to enjoy life. It is God, after all, "*who giveth us richly all things to enjoy.*" (1 Timothy 6:17b)

If a Christian has liberty, and what he does is not the primary issue of spirituality, then why are believers warned to avoid certain activities? The reason is because one cannot be carnal and spiritual at the same time. Many activities lead to carnality or cannot be done in accordance with the character of God. If a Christian is operating by the power of the flesh, he cannot at the same time be filled with the Spirit and bear fruit. One cannot, for example, kick the dog as unto the Lord.

> *Doth a fountain send forth at the same place sweet* water *and bitter? Can the fig tree, my brethren, bear olive berries? either a vine, figs? so* can *no fountain both yield salt water and fresh.* (James 3:11-12)

> *For they that are after the flesh do mind the things of the flesh; but they that are after the Spirit the things of the Spirit. For to be carnally minded* is *death; but to be spiritually minded* is *life and peace.* (Romans 8:5-6)

According to the Word, not According to My Soul

Spirituality has a particular information source; God's own word, the Bible. The spiritual man is filled with the Spirit because he lives in agreement with scripture, heeding its warnings to guard against unrighteousness. For example, he does not allow himself to dwell upon the past or upon things he cannot change; doing so only stirs up his soul, making him upset. When he seeks the support of fellow believers, he recognizes that godly fellowship can quickly become a forum for the flesh; He uses wisdom as to how much to share, and takes many of his cares only to the Lord. He balances his relationships with his godly calling to edify others and not to stumble them. His concern for his Christian brethren is a characteristic of his spiritual condition.

Brethren, I count not myself to have apprehended: but this one thing I do, forgetting those things which are behind, and reaching forth unto those things which are before, I press toward the mark for the prize of the high calling of God in Christ Jesus.
(Philippians 3:13-14)

So then every one of us shall give account of himself to God. Let us not therefore judge one another any more: but judge this rather, that no man put a stumblingblock or an occasion to fall in his brother's way ... Let us therefore follow after the things which make for peace, and things wherewith one may edify another.
(Romans 14:12-13, 19)

...be thou an example of the believers, in word, in conversation, in charity, in spirit, in faith, in purity. (1 Timothy 4:12b)

Let no unwholesome word proceed from your mouth, but only such a word as is good for edification according to the need of the moment, so that it will give grace to those who hear. (Ephesians 4:29 NASB)

...in lowliness of mind let each esteem other better than themselves. Look not every man on his own things, but every man also on the things of others. (Philippians 2:3b-4)

Sufficient, not Supplemental

Spirituality has a powerful tool; a sword that the Spirit uses to discern the Christian's mind and cut down his enemies (Ephesians 6:17). This sword, the Bible, claims to be sufficient for all things pertaining to life and godliness. Some subtly deny its sufficiency by saying that the Bible "contains" truth, meaning that additional or supplemental truth can be found somewhere else. There are many facts in the world, but truth is found only in God's word. To know the truth means to see things as they really are, and only God sees the truth of all things. The spiritual man is able to know, understand and implement the truths revealed in God's word to the extent that he studies and believes it. "Facts" often change as more is discovered, but truth is unchanging. The Bible's sufficiency does not mean that the Christian can go nowhere else for help or information. He might read books on parenting, or seek marital counseling, for example, but he does so by faith, utilizing wisdom. The information he gets does not replace scripture. He uses scripture to know whether and **how** to implement **what** he learns.

Believing in sufficiency means believing the Bible's own claims; it means to be persuaded that God has provided everything that His children need to know about Him in order to live according to His will without any deficiency. For any situation, the Bible has applicable wisdom; its contents are trustworthy and its teachings are unfailing. A spiritual man does not fit the Bible into the world; he filters the world through the Bible.

Yes, not No

See that ye refuse not him that speaketh. (Hebrews 12:25a)

The fruit of the Spirit facilitates a unique attitude toward life, people, and the world. Its hallmarks include the ability to say, "Yes," to God and to count everything that happens within the realm of spiritual living to be good. This is not to count sin or rebellion or evil as good. As an example, perhaps the spiritual man has an enemy with whom he would like to have words, but he knows that an argument would damage his testimony. Even though he feels a strong need for justice, he knows he is not to seek vengeance (Romans 12:9). The spiritual man chooses to trust God rather than to act according to his feelings. As his faith grows, it becomes easier for the spiritual man to hold his tongue. He sees himself maturing and others notice it too. This creates opportunities to explain the source of the changes and to share the Gospel of Christ, 1 Corinthians 15:1-4. Saying, "Yes," to God bore spiritual fruit that led to good works. As he builds experience with God's way of operating, the spiritual man counts things to be good even before he knows the results. He knows that God is always working for good, no matter how things appear, and in this he finds lasting peace.

Leading, not Divining

The doctrine of spirituality is a practical body of truth; it is living, active, and written in a book. Its purpose and use does not need to be "divined" from another source. It is doubtful that most Christians would intentionally practice divination, but some may do so unintentionally by attempting to read spiritual information into various thoughts, feelings, and circumstances. In such a case, mysticism or soulishness is mistaken for spirituality. What is known about God and His will is in the Bible. Part of Christian maturity is living with the reality that our heavenly Father doesn't tell us absolutely everything that we are to do. He provided a book of wisdom and a mechanism for thinking in accordance with Him. Part of what gives Him glory is that lowly human beings are actually able to use biblical wisdom to live righteously.

Biblical leading does not mean that God does not personally intervene in a Christian's life; we know that He does and the Bible says so. It does not mean that He does not answer prayers to open or close a door of opportunity. It simply means that we cannot make assumptions about feelings, dreams, open doors or anything else. Christians are to exercise wisdom and faith in uncertain situations just as they would at any other time.

The Spirit's leading is never said to be by way of an impression, a sensing, a feeling, or a sign. Like a coach leads a team, a general leads an army or a pastor leads a Bible study, instruction and training are provided to the members in order for them to achieve their goal.

*Howbeit when he, the Spirit of truth, is come, **he will guide you into all truth:** for he shall not speak of himself; but whatsoever* *he shall hear,* that *shall he speak: and he will shew you things to come.* (John 16:13, emphasis added)

It is not that God **cannot** verbally speak to us, or send a dream, or a feeling, or a prophetic messenger; that is not the issue. The issue is that God is the one who said His word is both sufficient and complete, and He does not contradict Himself. Denying sufficiency creates another problem. If one did receive something that he believes to be a sign, its source cannot be known; it could be a demon attempting to mislead. There is a reason that people continue to follow the pagan religions: when they pray to their "gods" for a sign, they occasionally do get one.

God's word is sure and safe. He protects us from lying signs by providing His revelation in writing. Each Christian must decide whether or not he believes that God's revelation is complete and not to be added to. Each must decide if he believes that scripture is living and active, ministered by the Holy Spirit to lead, teach, and correct. The dire danger that proceeds from the doctrine of "ongoing revelation" is that it makes the Bible utterly irrelevant. There is no sense at all to study what somebody else did 2000 years ago if personalized and current information can be had.

A spiritual man is led by the Spirit. Because he is rightly related to the Spirit, what he thinks, says and does is informed by the righteousness of God through His word. One who finds that he does not have access to God's wisdom and leading must ask himself how well he knows the scripture. How much time has he spent in study and memorization? The Holy Spirit needs something to use if He is to lead. A Christian needs to have God's truth in his mind in order for the Spirit to apply it to the situations of life. To have faith is to be persuaded, while sign-seeking is a mindset of uncertainty. The spiritual man does not need an answer for everything; he trusts God to bring about His outcomes in His perfect timing. He remembers that God *has* spoken—through His word.

> *He staggered not at the promise of God through unbelief; but was strong in faith, giving glory to God; And being fully persuaded that, what he had promised, he was able also to perform.* (Romans 4:20-21)

Liberty, not License

Spirituality is freedom, and only one who is born of the Spirit of God is truly free. Every human being is born enslaved to sin and can only produce things that are of a sinful quality. Only a spiritual man is free *not* to sin; he is empowered to withstand temptation. The spiritual man recognizes that his liberty in Christ is not for the purpose of returning to the domination of the sin principle within him, but is instead the freedom to enjoy all that God has given him to enjoy. Grace cannot possibly be a license to do whatever one wants. Any person, saved or unsaved, is already capable of doing whatever he wants. Grace is the enablement to do what God wants, something no unbeliever can do.

Consider the example of a young man reaching adulthood: he now considers himself free to do anything he wants, and he wants to do it all! He tries smoking, and soon finds that he has become a slave to an addiction. He overspends and becomes a slave to debt. He breaks the law, and finds he has limits placed on other liberties as well. What he thought of as freedom was actually the surrender of his freedom. Biblical freedom is not license; it is having the power *not* to sin.

...strengthened with all power, according to His glorious might,
for the attaining of all steadfastness and patience; joyously.
(Colossians 1:11 NASB)

When the spiritual man is tempted to do whatever he feels, or to say whatever is on his mind, if he wishes to maintain his spirituality, he must discern as to whether he can act in accordance with biblical liberty. He can ask himself whether it is possible to do what he desires as unto the Lord. If he cannot, the matter is not one of liberty. Although some fear that teaching grace encourages sin, exactly the opposite is true. If a Christian believes that he can sin more because he is operating under grace, then he needs more grace teaching, not less. He must learn that the faith system accesses power which enables him to live free from sin. That is biblical liberty.

It was for freedom that Christ set us free; therefore keep
standing firm and do not be subject again to a yoke of slavery.
(Galatians 5:1 NASB)

For, brethren, ye have been called unto liberty; only use not
liberty for an occasion to the flesh, but by love serve one another.
(Galatians 5:13)

Cooperation, not Independence

Spirituality is the result of a relationship. It has the character of a maturing child and his parent, in which the spiritual man lives in a state of informed reliance upon God, not in helplessness or ignorance. His time spent in God's word enables cooperation with God and willingness to make changes to his earthly life for the sake of the relationship. Sin is the outworking of independence from God, as exemplified by Adam and Eve. Eating fruit is not evil in itself; their sin was to act apart from God's stated will. They considered only their own desire and did not factor God into their decision except to doubt Him.

Cooperation is not only with God. The operation of the body of Christ is to be like that of a physical body, with each member working in unity and providing something that benefits the whole.

> ...from whom the whole body, being fitted and held together by what every joint supplies, according to the proper working of each individual part, causes the growth of the body for the building up of itself in love. (Ephesians 4:16 NASB)

The spiritual man asks himself things such as, "Is my attitude slipping? Is my motive right in this? Am I blinded by this wish?" His willingness to be critiqued allows the Holy Spirit to minister God's word to his conscience. The spiritual man can then come back into right adjustment with the Spirit if he has been entertaining carnal or deceptive thoughts. He is willing to allow the Spirit of God to change him, to correct him and to limit or stretch him as needed, so that he can work effectually as a member:

> For the word of God is quick, and powerful, and sharper than any two edged sword, piercing even to the dividing asunder of soul and spirit, and of the joints and marrow, and is a discerner of the thoughts and intents of the heart. (Hebrews 4:12)

> Let us therefore, as many as be perfect, be thus minded: and if in any thing ye be otherwise minded, God shall reveal even this unto you. (Philippians 3:15)

Unto God, not unto Men

Spiritual fruit-bearing has a particular motive which is to bring Glory to our most worthy God. The spiritual man is not only to do Christian works such as evangelism and Bible study; God asks him to do **everything** as if he is doing it for Him. He is, in fact, doing it all for Him, to bring Him glory. The spiritual man evaluates his motive, asking himself, for example, "Can I refuse to forgive as unto the Lord? Can I complain as unto the Lord? Can I be bitter as unto the Lord?" If he is to do all things as unto the Lord, and there is something that is impossible to do for God's glory, his conscience will tell him so; he does not need a law to tell him. The indwelling Holy Spirit teaches the spiritual man what is good and acceptable, and empowers him to do it.

And whatsoever ye do, do it *heartily, as to the Lord, and not unto men.* (Colossians 3:23)

And be not conformed to this world: but be ye transformed by the renewing of your mind, that ye may prove what is *that good, and acceptable, and perfect, will of God.* (Romans 12:2)

... that we should bring forth fruit unto God. (Romans 7:4b)

Gratitude, not Obligation

Spirituality operates with a particular assumption; it assumes that God is good, and that what He does and what He allows is also for the sake of good. That assumption on the part of the spiritual man facilitates trust, cooperation and thankfulness. The spiritual man recognizes his dislike of some of his responsibilities, but desires to honor God nonetheless. Before he begins, he sets his mind on things above, not to escape his work, but to empower it. He worships God for who He is, and praises Him for what He has done. As he yields to God, his "knowing" energizes his "doing" and he does his work without strife or resentment.

The spiritual man gives thanks "in Jesus' name," but this does not mean that he simply adds the phrase "in Jesus' name" onto the end of a prayer. The phrase, when stated, is a profession that the person praying is doing so in the Spirit. When a person acts in someone's name, he is representing him. A Christian represents Jesus when he allows Christlikeness to be displayed in him by the power of the Holy Spirit. In other words, a Christian is to be spiritual when giving thanks or doing anything else. When he is spiritual, he is functioning in accordance with the good name of Jesus Christ.

> And whatsoever ye do in word or deed, do all in the name of the Lord Jesus, giving thanks to God and the Father by him. (Colossians 3:17)

> Giving thanks always for all things unto God and the Father in the name of our Lord Jesus Christ. (Ephesians 5:20)

> In every thing give thanks: for this is the will of God in Christ Jesus concerning you. (1 Thessalonians 5:18)

> Rejoice always; pray without ceasing; in everything give thanks; for this is God's will for you in Christ Jesus. (1 Thessalonians 5:16-18 NASB)

Chapter 8

WHO CAN BE KNOWN
BY THEIR FRUITS?

Within the following passage from the Gospel of Matthew is the phrase, "Ye shall know them by their fruits." This verse is sometimes quoted by a church member who thinks that another member's unsatisfactory Christian performance indicates the lack of salvation. The person in question could be unsaved or he could be carnal and producing works of the flesh, but in either case, the verse is assumed to mean that works produced are the measure of one's salvation. This misuse of Matthew 7:16 is called "fruit-inspection" by some, and might be accompanied by the raised eyebrows of those who hope their "fruit" will not be the next to draw the eye of the inspector.

The topic of Matthew 7:15-23 is false prophets. Jesus is warning the nation of Israel about this important issue because sending prophets was the way in which God communicated with His people. The "fruit" of a prophet is prophecy; his prophecies were the declarations which he claimed were from God. The fruit described in this passage is not the spiritual fruit-bearing of the Christian.

Beware of false prophets, which come to you in sheep's clothing, but inwardly they are ravening wolves. Ye shall know them by their fruits. Do men gather grapes of thorns, or figs of thistles? Even so every good tree bringeth forth good fruit; but a corrupt tree bringeth forth evil fruit. A good tree cannot bring forth evil fruit, neither can a corrupt tree bring forth good fruit. Every tree that bringeth not forth good fruit is hewn down, and cast into the fire. Wherefore by their fruits ye shall know them. Not every one that saith unto me, Lord, Lord, shall enter into the kingdom of heaven; but he that doeth the will of my Father which is in heaven. Many will say to me in that day, Lord, Lord, have we not prophesied in thy name? and in thy name have cast out devils? and in thy name done many wonderful works? And then will I profess unto them, I never knew you: depart from me, ye that work iniquity. (Matthew 7:15-23)

Spirituality is Not in View

In the preceding passage, Jesus was not explaining to the church how to walk as a spiritual man, nor how to determine one's spiritual condition. Spirituality was not available as a normal part of a believer's experience until after the resurrection of Christ and the sending of the Holy Spirit. The walk of faith by the power of grace was not possible until sins were paid and God could come to indwell the forgiven and cleansed believer.

Making this distinction is not to deny that there are places in the Gospels of Matthew, Mark, Luke and John in which church teaching is foreshadowed. The general principle of the passage, that externals can be deceiving, has broad application. Even so, the particulars of Matthew 7 cannot be connected to salvation nor to spiritual fruit-bearing under grace. Moreover, spiritual fruit-bearing is spiritual and does not necessarily produce visible works. Likewise, salvation is by faith and is not visible.

What is Visible Can be Deceptive

Contrary to common usage, the "fruit" in Matthew 7 is not a visible product. Because they claimed to be prophets, the "fruit" of these men was not their works but their words, their alleged prophecies. They merely used their "wonderful works" to support their claim to be speaking for God. The outward activities of these false prophets seemed good; they appeared to be reproducing the works of Jesus Christ, casting out demons and more. The natural man can produce impressive works and show a convincing exterior, but both are counterfeit; they do not accurately reflect his internal condition.

Jesus described the deceptive display of false prophets as "sheep's clothing;" their works portrayed one thing while their words told a different story. If one looked only at the "clothing," meaning the outer appearance and activities of these men, one would come to an incorrect conclusion about them. Even the false prophets themselves seem to be deceived; they proudly boasted of their works and expressed surprise that they were not accepted. Apparently these men did not know that accurate beliefs must precede approved works. Jesus was warning Israel that being drawn in by works and other external indicators was a set-up to deception and to being destroyed by "wolves."

Their Beliefs, Not Their Works, Reveal the Truth

Although the word picture of a tree bearing fruit is used in this passage, the context reveals that the fruit being described is not the false prophets' works. It must be so because Jesus said that their falseness can be detected, but the external evidence, their "clothing," is not the way. "You will know them by their fruits" means that if one listened to what these so-called prophets were saying, one would know what they believed. By comparing the false prophets' proclamations to scripture, hearers would have been able to determine that these men did not believe in accordance with God's word. One who judged these men by their works would be deceived, but one who listened would recognize them as wolves. This is the biblical meaning of "fruit inspection," to look deeper than the outward performance of these deceivers.

The false prophets were not operating "in his name," but believed something contrary to God; therefore their works had the character of that lying source. Jesus described the quality of their works as "iniquity," meaning lawlessness. They were not operating by the principles given by God, nor were they doing His will. The first step in doing God's will must always be to know and believe what His word says.

Christians Are to Judge Doctrine

In regard to failure in the Christian life, Paul wrote that the works of the flesh are manifest; in other words, if someone is practicing sin, it can be seen. Adultery, drunkenness, and the other fleshly works listed in Galatians 5:19-21 are easily determined to be carnal and not spiritual in nature. This is not so, however, with good deeds, which can be done by well-meaning unbelievers. Such works are not of a godly quality and will not gain God's favor for the doers, but they are still "good" by human standards. Therefore, using only external factors is not a reliable way to make determinations about a person's spiritual condition. This begs the question as to whether Christians should be attempting to judge this at all. Yes, they must. The Bible calls for fellowship in the truth and among believers, and for evangelism of the unsaved (Romans 16:17, Hebrews 10:25, 2 Corinthians 6:14). Doing so would be impossible if one cannot tell who is who. There must be an effort made to learn what people know and believe, and that is done talking with them about truth and using discernment in regard to what is heard.

Making judgments in regard to sound doctrine is vital to the Christian life, just as making judgments about false prophets was vital to the nation of Israel in order to remain in the will of God under the law and the prophets. The fruit of the Christian is love, peace, joy, goodness, self-control, and many other spiritual qualities; they are to be the normal experience of the Christian, but they are not visible in the same way that works are. Because salvation comes by believing the Gospel of Christ, 1 Corinthians 15:1-4, judging a man's works to make determinations about his salvation will not provide a reliable answer. Learning what he believes is what will disclose his spiritual condition. The error of practicing "fruit inspection" among Christians can lead to hard feelings and self-righteousness; coming alongside the brother who seems to be struggling, however, fulfills the call to love God by loving His children.

Seeing ye have purified your souls in obeying the truth through the Spirit unto unfeigned love of the brethren, see that ye *love one another with a pure heart fervently...* (1 Peter 1:22)

Hereby perceive we the love of God, *because he laid down his life for us: and we ought to lay down* our *lives for the brethren.* (1 John 3:16)

HERE, ENJOY SOME FRUIT

It is common, commendable and expected for a new believer to be enthusiastic to please his Lord. Eager to obey God, he may begin trying to figure out what God wants him to **do**. Should I go on a mission trip? Should I teach Sunday school? Should I do more volunteer work? Would God like that? This is often "putting the cart before the horse." The new Christian is earnest and sincere, but may not yet know how to be spiritual. Doing works in the flesh can in some cases be worse than doing nothing at all. As he tries his best to please God, without the power of grace, he may fail, give up, or burn out, never returning to Christian living.

Every believer must learn to walk free from the law of sin, flee the siren call of this world and avoid the snares of the devil. To do so, he must first learn to be spiritual. The Christian who does will not only bear fruit, he will not become weary in well doing. It might seem counterintuitive to do so, but we, the authors, say again, to learn to be spiritual a Christian must shift his primary focus from wondering what to **do**, and focus instead on what God wants all of us to **know**. In keeping with that message, we have included a chapter full of even more verses about fruit. Noteworthy among them is the Hebrews passage, which after listing twenty characteristics of spiritual fruit, ends with good works, the last item on the list. It does not say, "Do good works and here is what you should do." It describes the outworking of spirituality so that a Christian's good works would be of a "perfect" quality, rightly adjusted for God's glory.

Writing about fruit reminded us of an acquaintance, who, after attending a study of 1 Thessalonians 5, was vocally upset over verse 17, "Pray without ceasing." He said, "I can't pray all day! I have to do my job!" This is an example of misunderstanding the unique nature of a spiritual relationship. Our intelligent, loving and practical God does not ask us to do what we cannot. He does not make us do what we do not want to do. We have heard people say that they feel like lesser Christians because they do not want to serve overseas. Others have said they are not aware of any special talent and fear that they cannot serve God. Some have resorted to praying for a sign because they had no idea what they are supposed to do in their Christian life. Rest easy, dear Christian. God is not trying to make His will mysterious or unsolvable, however it may seem. His yoke is so light that perhaps some of us cannot believe it. As we once heard it said, "God does everything for the believer except open the Bible."

When we learn to live a Spirit-filled life, what we find is glorious liberty, having dropped the yoke we have made for ourselves. Instead of beating up ourselves for not doing enough, or trying to figure out where to find the time to do more, or wracking our brains as to which things we are to do and whether God will be happy with them, we can enter the peaceful existence known as the believer's rest.

There remaineth therefore a rest to the people of God. For he that is entered into his rest, he also hath ceased from his own works, as God did from his. (Hebrews 4:9-10)

Much Fruit, with Emphasis Added

*But now being made free from sin, and become servants to God, ye have your fruit unto **holiness**, and the end everlasting life.* (Romans 6:22)

*For the fruit of the Spirit is in all **goodness and righteousness and truth**.* (Ephesians 5:9)

*For the hope which is laid up for you in heaven, whereof ye heard before in the word of the truth of the gospel; Which is come unto you, as it is in all the world; and bringeth forth fruit, as it doth also **in you**, since the day ye heard of it, and knew the grace of God in truth.* (Colossians 1:5-6)

*Now no chastening for the present seemeth to be joyous, but grievous: nevertheless afterward it yieldeth the **peaceable fruit of righteousness** unto them which are exercised thereby.* (Hebrews 12:11)

*But the wisdom that is from above is first pure, then peaceable, gentle, and easy to be intreated, full of mercy and good fruits, without partiality, and without hypocrisy. And the **fruit of righteousness** is sown in peace of them that make peace.* (James 3:17-18)

*That ye might walk worthy of the Lord unto all pleasing, being **fruitful in** every good work, and **increasing in the knowledge of God**.* (Colossians 1:10)

Every man according as he purposeth in his heart, so let him give;
*not grudgingly, or of necessity: for God loveth a cheerful giver.
And God* is *able to make all grace abound toward you; that ye,
always having all **sufficiency** in all* things, *may abound to **every
good work**: (As it is written, He hath dispersed abroad; he hath
given to the poor: his righteousness remaineth for ever. Now he
that ministereth seed to the sower both minister bread for* your
*food, and multiply your seed sown, and increase the **fruits of your
righteousness;)** Being enriched in every thing to all bountifulness,
which causeth **through us** thanksgiving to God.*
(2 Corinthians 9:7-11)

*1 Let brotherly **love** continue. 2 Be not*	Love
*forgetful to **entertain** strangers: for*	Hospitality/Openness
thereby some have entertained angels	
*unawares. 3 **Remember** them that are*	Consideration
in bonds, as bound with them; and	Empathy
them which suffer adversity, as being	Compassion
*yourselves also in the body. 4 **Marriage** is*	Purity
honourable in all, and the bed undefiled:	
but whoremongers and adulterers God	Self-Control
will judge. 5 Let *your conversation* be	
without covetousness; and be ***content***	Contentment
with such things as ye have: for he hath	
said, I will never leave thee, nor forsake	
*thee. 6 So that we may **boldly** say, The*	Confidence
Lord is *my helper, and I will **not fear***	Courage
what man shall do unto me. 7 Remember	
them which have the rule over you, who	

have spoken unto you the word of God:
whose faith follow, *considering the end
of their conversation. 8 **Jesus Christ** the
same yesterday, and to day, and for ever.
9 Be not carried about with divers and
strange doctrines. For it is a good thing
that the heart be **established** with grace;
not with meats, which have not **profited**
them that have been occupied therein. 10
We have an altar, whereof they have no
right to eat which serve the tabernacle.
11 For the bodies of those beasts, whose
blood is brought into the sanctuary by the
high priest for sin, are burned without the
camp. 12 Wherefore Jesus also, that he
might **sanctify** the people with his own
blood, suffered without the gate. 13 Let
us **go forth therefore unto him** without
the camp, **bearing his reproach**. 14 For
here have we no continuing city, but we
seek one to come. 15 By him therefore
let us offer the sacrifice of **praise** to God
continually, that is, the fruit of our lips
giving thanks to his name. 16 But to
do **good** and to **communicate** forget
not: for with such **sacrifices** God is well
pleased. 17 **Obey** them that have the
rule over you, and **submit** yourselves: for
they watch for your souls, as they that*

Maturity
Faith

Doctrinal fidelity
Stability
Reward is in view

Holiness

Separation from sin
Identification with
Christ
Hope
Praise

Gratitude
Helping/Fellowship
Includes giving
Obedience
Submission to authority

*must give account, that they may do it
with joy, and not with grief: for that is
unprofitable for you. 18 Pray for us: for
we trust we have a **good conscience**, in
all things willing to live **honestly**. 19 But
I beseech you the rather to do this, that
I may be restored to you the sooner. 20
Now the God of **peace**, that brought again
from the dead our Lord Jesus, that great
shepherd of the sheep, through the blood
of the everlasting covenant, 21 Make you
perfect in **every good work** to do his will,
working in you that which is wellpleasing
in his sight, through Jesus Christ; to whom
be **glory** for ever and ever. Amen. 22 And
I beseech you, brethren, suffer the word
of **exhortation**: for I have written a letter
unto you in few words.* (Hebrews 13:1-22)

Godliness

Reward is in view
Good conscience
Honesty

Peace
Power

Good works are last
on the list, produced
in us, by Him, for His
glory.

I am holding up truth
to you—say, "Yes," to it!

Notes

Bearing Fruit or Living Barren

Bearing Fruit or Living Barren

Other books from Sufficient Word Publishing

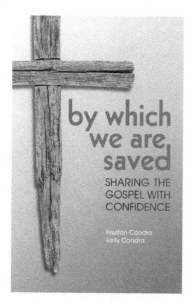

Bear much fruit in your faith and enrich your relationship with God

By Which We Are Saved is a complete handbook for witnessing and fully equips the Christian for positive interactions and effective evangelism.

The Gospel of Christ is a message which claims to save from damnation those who believe it.

This "good news" message purports to reveal who saves, what he did, why we need it, how we get it, and where to find reliable information about it. Using Bible verses, *"I Have Some Good News"* addresses objections to the Gospel, and allows Christianity's source book to speak for itself.

Contact us at publisher@sufficientwordpublishing.com about
Preston and Kelly Condra speaking at your church or conference.

CPSIA information can be obtained
at www.ICGtesting.com
Printed in the USA
BVHW04s0456270818
525379BV00008B/40/P